A Comprehensive Practice Book
for School Olympiads & Talent Search Exams

COMPUTER
Class 6

by
Sanjib Pal

Bloom Cap Edu Ventures Pvt. Ltd.

Administrative & Production Office

'Ramchhaya' 4577/15, Agarwal Road, Darya Ganj, New Delhi -110002
Tele: 011- 47630600, 43518550

PRICE: ₹125.00

PO No : TXT-XX-XXXXXXX-X-XX

Published by Arihant Publications (I) Ltd.

For further information about the books log on to
www.bloomcap.org

Follow us on   

Preface

"Future belongs to those Who prepares for it today"

School Olympiads are National & International level competitions conducted by different Government, Non-Government & Educational Organisations with the purpose of making the children ready to face competitive exams.

The challenging Questions asked in Olympiads motivate them to learn more & more and bring out the best result with improved academic performance. The Awards & Scholarship offered by Olympiads motivate children to aspire & strive for doing better and emerge out to be the best.

Science Olympiads

Being a Scientist or Engineer or Doctor has always been a dream of each school going child. A good command over Science is a must for any of these. Questions of Science Olympiads are structured to help students to develop scientific temperament & motivate them to understand the concepts of science. They also focuses on improving existing knowledge of a student by adding more information.

'Bloom Science Olympiad Study Book Class 6' is a perfect resource to Study & Practice for Olympiad Exams and other National & State Level Talent Search Exams & Other Competitions.

Some Special Features of Bloom Science Olympiad Study Books are;

- Chapterwise Exercises having different types of Objective Questions; Analytical, Applications, Remembering etc, at par with the Olympiad Level.
- Detailed Explanation for each question.
- Olympiad Pattern Practice Sets at the end.

This book is prepared by Expert Panel with the utmost care, still if you have any suggestions regarding its improvement then feel free to contact us at support@bloomcap.org. We will try to inculcate your suggestions in the further editions.

Contents

Fundamentals of Computer

MCQs 1 Mark Questions

1. What is the full form of Computer?
   (a) Commonly Operated Machine Purposely Used for Technological and Educational Research
   (b) Computational, Operational and Programming Machine
   (c) Common Operating System for Programming and Technical Research
   (d) Computational Programming Machine Usable for Technical Research

2. The first automatic electronic digital computer was called
   (a) ENIAC
   (b) UNIVAC
   (c) Mark-I
   (d) ABC

3. .... is known as the Father of Computers.
   (a) Charles Babbage
   (b) Von Neumann
   (c) Pascal
   (d) Newton

4. Which of the following types of computers uses EBCDIC?
   (a) Supercomputers
   (b) Mainframe computers
   (c) Minicomputers
   (d) Microcomputers

5. Where are the critical parts of a desktop PC located?
   (a) Hard disk (b) CPU
   (c) UPS (d) Monitor

6. The data given to a computer is converted into electrical signals by which type of devices?
   (a) Output devices
   (b) Input devices
   (c) Memory devices
   (d) Both (a) and (b)

7. A computer gets power through which of the following devices?
   (a) CPU
   (b) SMPS
   (c) Powerboard
   (d) Monitor

8. Identify the name of the missing units in the given diagram (in chronological order).

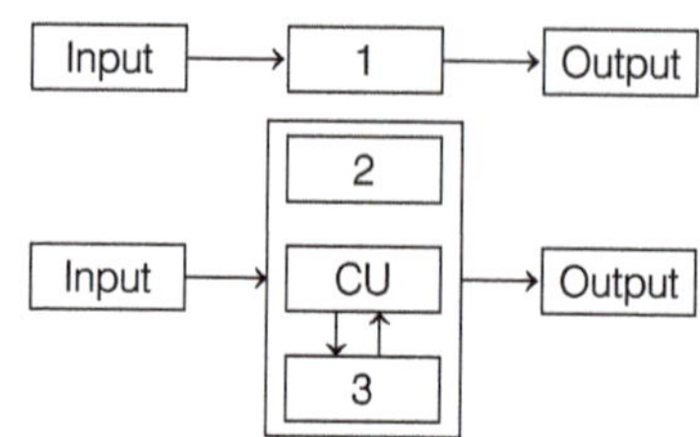

(a) 1-Compiler, 2 Memory, 3 CPU
(b) 1-Process, 2 Storage, 3 ALU
(c) 1-Media, 2 IC, 3 ALU
(d) 1-Process, 2 ALU, 3 Storage

9. Which computer component is made up of a semiconductor material called silicon?
(a) Keyboard
(b) CRT
(c) Microprocessor
(d) None of the above

10. In which unit, the actual computations take place?
(a) Control Unit (b) ALU
(c) Memory Unit (d) None of these

11. There are many devices which can be connected to a computer but they are not a part of core computer architecture. What are these devices called?
(a) Memory Devices
(b) Control Unit
(c) Peripheral Devices
(d) USB

12. Which tool or software program checks for bugs in other programs?
(a) Compiler (b) Interpreter
(c) Debugger (d) All of these

13. Find the odd one out.
(a) Bit (b) Nibble
(c) Byte (d) Hertz

14. A computer can perform multiple tasks at the same time. What is this ability called?
(a) Speed (b) Versatility
(c) Diligence (d) Accuracy

15. Which of the following is not a feature of computer?
(a) Speed (b) Economy
(c) Accuracy (d) Versatility

16. Which feature of a computer ensures that we can trust the output given by the computer?
(a) Reliability (b) Diligence
(c) Accuracy (d) Versatility

17. Which of the following options has a chronologically correct order?
(a) Input-Output-Storage-Memory
(b) Input-Storage-Process-Output
(c) Input-Process-Output-Storage
(d) Input-Memory-Output

18. Air conditioners, washing machines, ATMs, etc., all have in-built computers. What type of computers are these?
(a) Minicomputer
(b) Embedded computer
(c) Supercomputer
(d) Mainframe computer

19. Which of the following is an incorrect type of computer on the basis of data handling capability?
(a) Digital (b) Analog
(c) Remote (d) Hybrid

20. .... is the most common type of computer.
(a) Microcomputer
(b) Minicomputer
(c) Supercomputer
(d) Mainframe computer

21. Which of the following was the first laptop computer?
(a) IBM PC
(b) Osborne 1
(c) Epson HX 20
(d) Epson L3S

22. .... is a supercomputer capable of offering a peak performance of 838 teraflops.
(a) PARAM Siddhi
(b) PARAM Shivay
(c) PARAM Ananta
(d) PARAM Shakti

23. Which of the following is a series of supercomputers designed & developed by Bhabha Atomic Research Centre for their internal usages?
(a) Anupam (b) PARAM
(c) Aaditya (d) Fugaku

24. Frontier, the world's fastest supercomputer is built by
(a) CDAC (b) Epson
(c) HPE (d) IBM

25. Which of the following types of computers is small, less expensive and less powerful?
(a) Microcomputer
(b) Minicomputer
(c) Mainframe computer
(d) Supercomputer

26. Government needs a machine for heavy scientific and engineering purposes such as aerodynamics, weather forecasting, nuclear fusion research, etc. Which computer will be the best to perform such operations?
(a) Microcomputer
(b) Minicomputer
(c) Supercomputer
(d) Mainframe computer

27. .... is a type of a minicomputer.
(a) Commodore 64
(b) ENIAC
(c) Honeywell 200
(d) Cray

MCQs 2 Mark Questions

28. This was the first commercially successful minicomputer. Identify it.

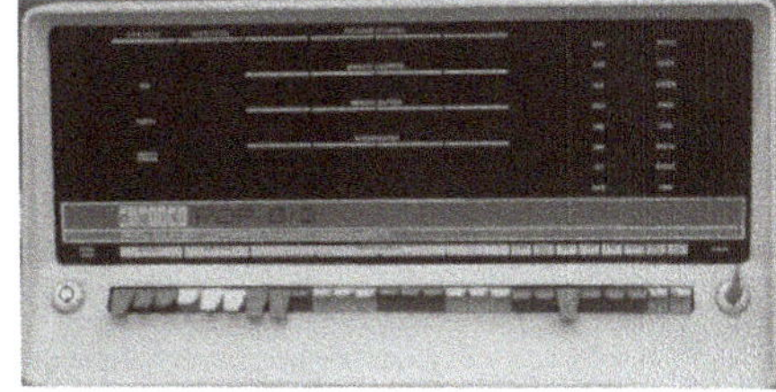

(a) Commodore 64
(b) ANURAG
(c) PDP-8
(d) PARAM

29. Identify the correct statement(s).
I. The speed of a mainframe computer is measured in MIPS.
II. Tablet computer is a kind of microcomputer.

Codes
(a) Only I
(b) Only II
(c) Both I and II
(d) Neither I nor II

30. Identify X according to the given statement.
X is used to translate the program written in assembly language to machine language.
(a) Compiler (b) Assembler
(c) Interpreter (d) Debugger

31. Read the given statements carefully and identify the name of the computer.

I. It was the first electronic computer used for solving numerical problems.

II. It generated a lot of heat that resulted in its malfunctioning.

(a) ENIAC (b) UNIVAC

(c) IBM 650 (d) EDVAC

32. Match the following lists.

List I (Name of Computer)	**List II** (Type)
A. Trinity	1. A US supercomputer built by National Nuclear Security Administration (NNSA) for the Advanced Simulation and Computing Program (ASC).
B. PARAM Yuva II	2. A programmable electronic and digital computer developed by Tommy Flowers.
C. Colossus	3. A supercomputer developed by CDAC.

Codes

	A	B	C
(a)	2	3	1
(b)	3	2	1
(c)	3	1	2
(d)	1	3	2

33. Identify X and Y from the given statements.

X	Y
It converts high level language to low level language.	It also converts high level language to low level language.
It reads the program line by line and then does the processing and execution.	It reads the whole program, processes it and executes it in a one go.
The translation is done one statement at a time.	The translation of the entire program is done in one go.

(a) X : Debugger Y : Compiler

(b) X : Compiler Y : Debugger

(c) X : Interpreter Y : Compiler

(d) X : Compiler Y: Interpreter

Darken your choice with HB Pencil

1.	ⓐ ⓑ ⓒ ⓓ	7.	ⓐ ⓑ ⓒ ⓓ	13.	ⓐ ⓑ ⓒ ⓓ	19.	ⓐ ⓑ ⓒ ⓓ	25.	ⓐ ⓑ ⓒ ⓓ	31.	ⓐ ⓑ ⓒ ⓓ
2.	ⓐ ⓑ ⓒ ⓓ	8.	ⓐ ⓑ ⓒ ⓓ	14.	ⓐ ⓑ ⓒ ⓓ	20.	ⓐ ⓑ ⓒ ⓓ	26.	ⓐ ⓑ ⓒ ⓓ	32.	ⓐ ⓑ ⓒ ⓓ
3.	ⓐ ⓑ ⓒ ⓓ	9.	ⓐ ⓑ ⓒ ⓓ	15.	ⓐ ⓑ ⓒ ⓓ	21.	ⓐ ⓑ ⓒ ⓓ	27.	ⓐ ⓑ ⓒ ⓓ	33.	ⓐ ⓑ ⓒ ⓓ
4.	ⓐ ⓑ ⓒ ⓓ	10.	ⓐ ⓑ ⓒ ⓓ	16.	ⓐ ⓑ ⓒ ⓓ	22.	ⓐ ⓑ ⓒ ⓓ	28.	ⓐ ⓑ ⓒ ⓓ		
5.	ⓐ ⓑ ⓒ ⓓ	11.	ⓐ ⓑ ⓒ ⓓ	17.	ⓐ ⓑ ⓒ ⓓ	23.	ⓐ ⓑ ⓒ ⓓ	29.	ⓐ ⓑ ⓒ ⓓ		
6.	ⓐ ⓑ ⓒ ⓓ	12.	ⓐ ⓑ ⓒ ⓓ	18.	ⓐ ⓑ ⓒ ⓓ	24.	ⓐ ⓑ ⓒ ⓓ	30.	ⓐ ⓑ ⓒ ⓓ		

History and Generations of Computer

MCQs 1 Mark Questions

1. Which of the following was an electronic computer in which a program was stored for the first time?
   (a) Cray-1 (b) Epson HX20
   (c) ENIAC (d) Difference engine

2. The basic principle of which device is still used in modern day water meters and odometers?
   (a) Abacus
   (b) Pascal's calculator
   (c) Napier's bones
   (d) Mark I

3. Which family of computers varies from small to large in size and is capable of performing commercial and scientific computations?
   (a) ABC (b) UNIVAC
   (c) ENIAC (d) IBM System/360

4. .... was an electromechanical computer.
   (a) Mark I (b) Epson L3S
   (c) Deep blue (d) IBM 1401

5. .... were used for storage in Hollerith's Machine.
   (a) Punched cards (b) ICs
   (c) Microprocessor (d) Magnetic tape

6. Tabulating Machine Company, established in 1896 was renamed as .... in ....
   (a) Microsoft,1924 (b) IBM,1924
   (c) Facebook,1923 (d) Apple,1920

7. .... was used as a programming language in second generation.
   (a) BASIC (b) QBASIC
   (c) FORTRAN (d) PASCAL

8. Identify the component that was used in the first generation computers.
   (a) Microprocessor (b) Vacuum tubes
   (c) Transistor (d) ICs

9. .... and .... were used as storage devices in third generation.
   (a) Magnetic tape, magnetic disk
   (b) Magnetic tape, transistor
   (c) Magnetic disk, punched cards
   (d) Magnetic tape, hard disk

10. Which third generation computer used binary digits to represent numbers and data?

(a) Mark I (b) EDSAC
(c) ABC (d) Honeywell 6000

11. Which technology helped in developing very small but extremely powerful and fast computers known as ROBOTS?

(a) VLSI (b) SSI
(c) MSI (d) ULSI

12. .... was the first ever popularly used tablet computer.

(a) Cray-1
(b) UNIVAC
(c) Epson HX
(d) iPad

13. Find the odd one out.

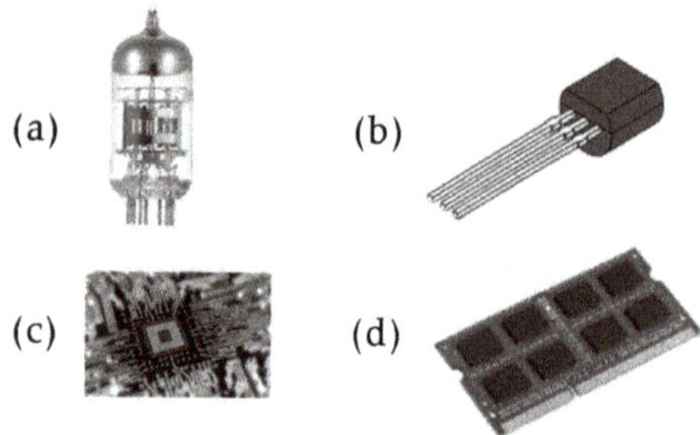

14. Arrange the following computers in the chronological order of the generations in which they were developed.

(a) UNIVAC, IBM1620, IBM 360, Apple Macintosh, MacBook Pro
(b) UNIVAC, IBM 360, Apple Macintosh, MacBook Pro, IBM1620
(c) IBM 360, UNIVAC, Apple Macintosh, MacBook Pro, IBM1620
(d) Apple Macintosh, UNIVAC, MacBook Pro, IBM1620, IBM 360

15. UNIVAC III and CDC 1604 belong to .... generation of computers.

(a) First (b) Second
(c) Fourth (d) Third

16. .... was the main concept behind the improved computation power and reduced size of fourth generation computers.

(a) Artificial intelligence
(b) Microprocessor
(c) Magnetic disk
(d) Integrated circuits

17. Identify the device according to the given description.

- It was the first electronic computer invented in 1946 by John Presper Eckert and John Mauchly.
- It was used for general purposes, such as solving numerical problems.
- It stored maximum 20 numbers in its internal memory and used around 18000 vacuum tubes.
- It was about 1000 times faster than relay computers but generated a lot of heat.

(a) EDVAC (b) UNIVAC
(c) ENIAC (d) EDSAC

18. The given logo is of a company which makes home video game consoles. Identify the company and the computer generation on which these games are based.

(a) Nintendo, First
(b) Commodore 64, Third
(c) Windows 10, First
(d) Playstation, Fifth

19. Identify the computer generation from the following information.

- AI based systems
- ULSI was introduced
- Deep blue –the first chess playing computer was developed by IBM.

(a) First (b) Third
(c) Second (d) Fifth

MCQs 2 Mark Questions

20. Arrange the following computers in increasing order of their speed.

I. Honeywell 6000
II. Epson HX20
III. EDSAC
IV. IBM 7094

Codes

(a) I, II, III, IV (b) I, III, II, IV
(c) II, I, III, IV (d) III, IV, II, I

21. Which of the following statements are true about Apple Macintosh?

I. It is a fourth generation family of computers designed, manufactured and sold by Apple since January 1984.
II. The original Mac was the first mass-marketed personal computer that featured a graphical interface, built-in screen and mouse.

Codes

(a) Only I (b) Only II
(c) Neither I nor II (d) Both I and II

22. Identify this machine capable of reading both numbers and characters and giving the output in desired format. It used electricity and was also known as the punched cards machine. Also, name the inventor of this machine.

(a) Difference engine, Babbage
(b) Analytical engine, Babbage
(c) Napier's bones, John Napier
(d) Hollerith's Machine, Herman Hollerith

23. Match the following lists.

	Machine		**Name**
A.		1.	Napier's bones
B.		2.	Pascal's Adding machine
C.		3.	Difference engine
D.		4.	Analytical engine

Codes

	A	B	C	D		A	B	C	D
(a)	3	1	4	2	(b)	2	1	4	3
(c)	2	4	3	1	(d)	4	3	2	1

24. Match the following lists.

	List I		**List II**
A.	Baby	1.	First mass produced computer
B.	Pascal's calculator	2.	Los Alamos installed at National Lab.
C.	IBM 650	3.	First graphical computer game
D.	Cray-1	4.	Totally automatic mechanical device

Codes

	A	B	C	D		A	B	C	D
(a)	2	1	4	3	(b)	3	4	1	2
(c)	2	3	1	4	(d)	1	4	3	2

25. Given below are the images of two components that were used in different computer generations along with their examples.

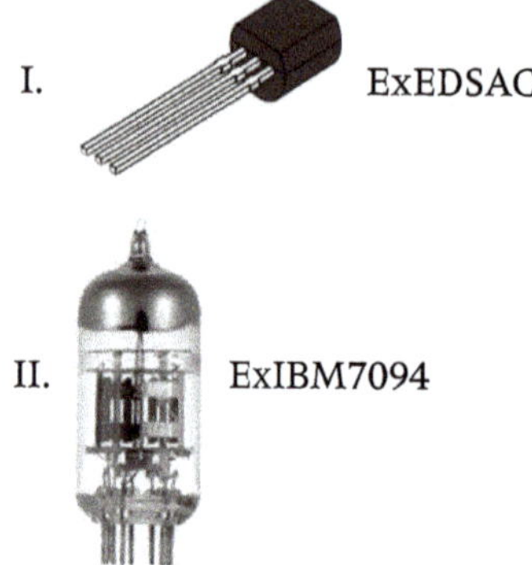

Identify the generations, storage and languages used in those devices.

(a) (I) First generation, Magnetic drum, Machine language (II) Second generation, Magnetic tape, FORTRAN

(b) (I) Second generation, Magnetic tape, FORTRAN (II) First generation, Magnetic drum, Machine language

(c) (I) Third generation, Magnetic disk, COBOL (II) First generation, Magnetic tape, FORTRAN

(d) (I) Fourth generation, CD, Binary language (II) Second generation, Hard disk, QBASIC

26. Which of the following statements is incorrect about third generation of computers?

I. In third generation, computer transistors were replaced with Integrated Circuits.

II. LSI and VLSI technology were used in this generation to enhance the speed of computers.

III. The storage devices used in this generation were transistors and vacuum tubes.

Codes

(a) I and II

(b) II and III

(c) I and III

(d) All of the above

Darken your choice with HB Pencil

1.	ⓐ ⓑ ⓒ ⓓ	**6.**	ⓐ ⓑ ⓒ ⓓ	**11.**	ⓐ ⓑ ⓒ ⓓ	**16.**	ⓐ ⓑ ⓒ ⓓ	**21.**	ⓐ ⓑ ⓒ ⓓ	**26.**	ⓐ ⓑ ⓒ ⓓ
2.	ⓐ ⓑ ⓒ ⓓ	**7.**	ⓐ ⓑ ⓒ ⓓ	**12.**	ⓐ ⓑ ⓒ ⓓ	**17.**	ⓐ ⓑ ⓒ ⓓ	**22.**	ⓐ ⓑ ⓒ ⓓ		
3.	ⓐ ⓑ ⓒ ⓓ	**8.**	ⓐ ⓑ ⓒ ⓓ	**13.**	ⓐ ⓑ ⓒ ⓓ	**18.**	ⓐ ⓑ ⓒ ⓓ	**23.**	ⓐ ⓑ ⓒ ⓓ		
4.	ⓐ ⓑ ⓒ ⓓ	**9.**	ⓐ ⓑ ⓒ ⓓ	**14.**	ⓐ ⓑ ⓒ ⓓ	**19.**	ⓐ ⓑ ⓒ ⓓ	**24.**	ⓐ ⓑ ⓒ ⓓ		
5.	ⓐ ⓑ ⓒ ⓓ	**10.**	ⓐ ⓑ ⓒ ⓓ	**15.**	ⓐ ⓑ ⓒ ⓓ	**20.**	ⓐ ⓑ ⓒ ⓓ	**25.**	ⓐ ⓑ ⓒ ⓓ		

Hardware and Software

MCQs 1 Mark Questions

1. .... refer to the parts of a computer that we can touch and feel.
   (a) Hardware (b) Software
   (c) Firmware (d) Liveware

2. Which of the following is not a computer hardware?
   (a) Keyboard (b) MS Word
   (c) CPU (d) Monitor

3. .... is the central backbone of a computer on which other parts are installed.
   (a) Memory (b) Motherboard
   (c) Monitor (d) UPS

4. A computer display is an arrangement of pixels in a horizontal and vertical manner. What is this arrangement called?
   (a) Resolution (b) Screen
   (c) Display (d) Monitor

5. A .... cannot be used while connecting a peripheral device to a computer.
   (a) USB (b) BIOS
   (c) Serial port (d) Parallel port

6. Find the odd one out.

(a) 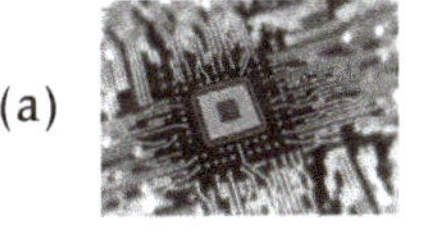
(b) 
(c) 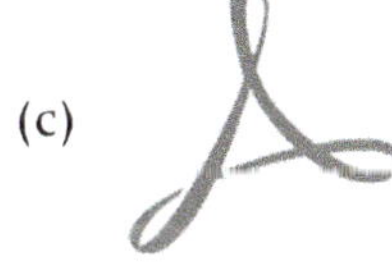
(d) 

7. The CPU clock speed is measured in
   (a) bits per second
   (b) bytes per second
   (c) gigahertz, megahertz
   (d) terahertz

8. Which of the following is/are pointing devices?
   (a) Mouse (b) Trackball
   (c) Joystick (d) All of these

9. Seema wants to take a hard copy of an image saved on her computer. Which device will be used to do the same?
   (a) Plotter (b) Printer
   (c) Scanner (d) Monitor

10. Which of the following is used to verify the authenticity of paper documents especially cheques?

(a) ORM (b) OCR
(c) MICR (d) OMR

11. Identify the given device which provides input and output of audio signals to and from a computer under the control of computer programs?

(a) A graphics card
(b) A sound card
(c) A memory card
(d) Motherboard

12. Wireless mouse communicates through

(a) infrared waves
(b) microwaves
(c) radio waves
(d) electromagnetic waves

13. .... is a device through which we can directly point and select objects on the display screen.

(a) Mouse (b) Trackball
(c) Light pen (d) Both (a) and (b)

14. The given image is of an output from a printer. Can you identify the printer which prints the output in the given form?

ABCDEFGHIJKLMNOP
QRSTUVWXYZÀÅÉÎÕa
bcdefghijklmnopqr
stuvwxyzàåéîõ&12
34567890($£€.,!?)

(a) Laser printer
(b) Inkjet printer
(c) Plotter
(d) Dot matrix printer

15. Which of the following devices will be used to read the code shown below?

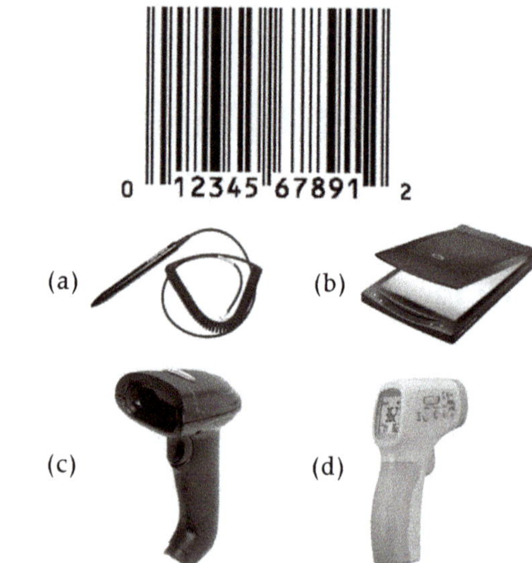

16. A computer has .... and .... memory.

(a) PROM, EEPROM
(b) Data, Input
(c) Internal, External
(d) Hard disk drive, Pen drive

17. Which of the following acts as the main memory of a computer?

(a) Motherboard
(b) Primary memory
(c) Operating system
(d) Secondary memory

18. Which of the following is a permanent memory and is also known as Auxiliary memory?

(a) Secondary memory
(b) SRAM
(c) DRAM/Registers
(d) Cache memory

19. Which of the following is the main and usually the largest data storage devices in a computer?
(a) CD (b) Hard disk drive
(c) Floppy disk (d) Magnetic tape

20. Gig stick, jump drive, disk key are all other names for
(a) Optical disk (b) Memory card
(c) USB Flash drive (d) Floppy disk

21. Which memory is also known as CPU memory and can be accessed by a microprocessor more quickly than RAM?
(a) Hard disk (b) ROM
(c) DRAM (d) Cache memory

22. SRAM, DRAM belong to which category of storage devices?
(a) Hard disks
(b) Pen drives
(c) Optical disks
(d) Random Access Memory

23. Which type of memory allows you to change its contents once after its manufacture and the data you enter is then permanent?
(a) ROM (b) EEPROM
(c) RAM (d) PROM

24. A zip disk when launched has a storage capacity of about
(a) 1 GB (b) 10 MB
(c) 150 MB (d) 100 MB

25. Which among the following is an optical storage device?

(a) 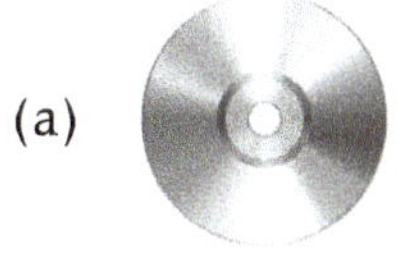 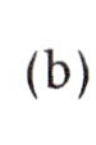 (b) 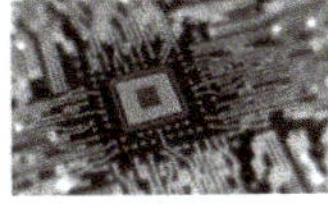

(c)  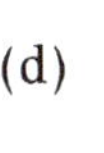 (d) 

26. Which of the following devices is a volatile storage device?

(a)  (b) 

(c)  (d) 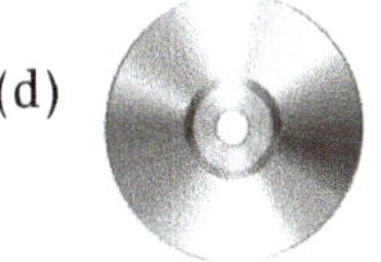

27. The given icon depicts a program which provides online file Hosting service. What is the name of this program?

(a) Google drive (b) Drop box
(c) Trash can (d) Desktop

28. The given image is of a device which uses laser light to read or write data on an optical disc. Identify the device.

(a) WiFi (b) Optical Disk Drive
(c) Bluetooth (d) Hard disk

29. A set of programs and associated documentation and configuration of data is known as
(a) Software
(b) Output
(c) Hardware
(d) None of the above

30. Which of the following acts as an interface between the hardware and the user?
(a) Memory
(b) Operating system software
(c) Keyboard
(d) Application software

31. System, application and utility are all types of
(a) hardware (b) software
(c) memory (d) microcomputer

32. A software program developed for performing particular tasks related to managing computer resources is called
(a) Application software
(b) System software
(c) Utility software
(d) Helper software

33. Ram wants to secure his computer from malware. What software should he use?
(a) Linux (b) Antivirus software
(c) Backup software (d) Windows

34. Student Record Software will be which type of software from among the following?
(a) Utility software
(b) Application software
(c) System software
(d) Operating system software

35. .... and .... are types of application software.
(a) Windows, MAC (b) Monitor, CPU
(c) Antivirus, backup (d) Adobe, Firefox

36. The given picture is of an application software program. Choose the option which describes the use of the given software correctly.

(a) Speaker (b) Media player
(c) Antivirus (d) Backup of data

MCQs 2 Mark Questions

37. Choose the option which depicts the correct chronological order of units of storage.
(a) nibble<byte<KB<bit<GB<MB<TB
(b) byte<bit<nibble<MB<GB<KB<TB
(c) bit<nibble<byte<KB<MB<GB<TB
(d) bit<byte<nibble<GB<KB<MB<TB

38. There is a relationship among different softwares, X and Y. Read the given statements carefully and identify X and Y.
I. X is a component which interacts with the operating system and can be touched and felt.
II. Y interacts with the application software directly and cannot see the background working of X.
(a) X : Device driver Y : Windows
(b) X : Storage Y : Hardware
(c) X : User Y : Hardware
(d) X : Hardware Y : User

39. Identify P and Q from the given statements.
I. P is a class of data storage devices that reads stored data in a sequence.
II. P can be magnetic storage or optical storage.
III. Q is a class of storage in which we can access data in any random order.
(a) P : Sequential Access Memory (SAM)
Q : Non-Sequential Memory
(b) P : Non-Sequential Memory
Q : Sequential Memory
(c) P : Hardware Q : Software
(d) P : Software Q : Hardware

40. Which of the following pair is incorrect?

	Memory	Storage
I.	A physical device in which data is stored permanently.	A physical device in which data is stored temporarily.
II.	Allows processor to access data to run applications and switch between various applications.	Allows storing and accessing files and applications.
III.	It is volatile and slow.	It is non-volatile and fast.

Codes
(a) Only I
(b) II and III
(c) Only III
(d) None of the above

41. Which of the following keys are not correctly matched to their functions?

Keys	Function
I. Escape key	Abort, cancel or close an operation
II. Shift key	To type a single capital letter and change the top number keys to a symbol
III. End key	Move the cursor to the end of a line or move to the bottom of a webpage
IV. Function key	Cursor control keys

Codes

(a) I, II and III (b) Only II
(c) III, I and II (d) Only IV

42. Which of the following devices are not correctly matched to their functions?

Device	Function
I. Storage	An output device used by a music software
II. Monitor	Example of output device
III. System software	Manages a computer and coordinates the functioning of hardware components
IV. Speaker	Example of an input device

Codes

(a) I and II (b) Only III
(c) III, IV and II (d) I and IV

43. Match the following lists.

List I (Device)	**List II** (Type)
A.	1. It allows us to design, edit and work upon a text file.
B.	2. It is hardware that contains major components of a computer.
C.	3. A type of volatile memory.
D.	4. These are different Input/output devices.

Codes

	A	B	C	D
(a)	3	1	2	4
(b)	3	2	4	1
(c)	2	3	4	1
(d)	3	4	2	1

Darken your choice with HB Pencil

1.	ⓐ ⓑ ⓒ ⓓ	9.	ⓐ ⓑ ⓒ ⓓ	17.	ⓐ ⓑ ⓒ ⓓ	25.	ⓐ ⓑ ⓒ ⓓ	33.	ⓐ ⓑ ⓒ ⓓ	41.	ⓐ ⓑ ⓒ ⓓ
2.	ⓐ ⓑ ⓒ ⓓ	10.	ⓐ ⓑ ⓒ ⓓ	18.	ⓐ ⓑ ⓒ ⓓ	26.	ⓐ ⓑ ⓒ ⓓ	34.	ⓐ ⓑ ⓒ ⓓ	42.	ⓐ ⓑ ⓒ ⓓ
3.	ⓐ ⓑ ⓒ ⓓ	11.	ⓐ ⓑ ⓒ ⓓ	19.	ⓐ ⓑ ⓒ ⓓ	27.	ⓐ ⓑ ⓒ ⓓ	35.	ⓐ ⓑ ⓒ ⓓ	43.	ⓐ ⓑ ⓒ ⓓ
4.	ⓐ ⓑ ⓒ ⓓ	12.	ⓐ ⓑ ⓒ ⓓ	20.	ⓐ ⓑ ⓒ ⓓ	28.	ⓐ ⓑ ⓒ ⓓ	36.	ⓐ ⓑ ⓒ ⓓ		
5.	ⓐ ⓑ ⓒ ⓓ	13.	ⓐ ⓑ ⓒ ⓓ	21.	ⓐ ⓑ ⓒ ⓓ	29.	ⓐ ⓑ ⓒ ⓓ	37.	ⓐ ⓑ ⓒ ⓓ		
6.	ⓐ ⓑ ⓒ ⓓ	14.	ⓐ ⓑ ⓒ ⓓ	22.	ⓐ ⓑ ⓒ ⓓ	30.	ⓐ ⓑ ⓒ ⓓ	38.	ⓐ ⓑ ⓒ ⓓ		
7.	ⓐ ⓑ ⓒ ⓓ	15.	ⓐ ⓑ ⓒ ⓓ	23.	ⓐ ⓑ ⓒ ⓓ	31.	ⓐ ⓑ ⓒ ⓓ	39.	ⓐ ⓑ ⓒ ⓓ		
8.	ⓐ ⓑ ⓒ ⓓ	16.	ⓐ ⓑ ⓒ ⓓ	24.	ⓐ ⓑ ⓒ ⓓ	32.	ⓐ ⓑ ⓒ ⓓ	40.	ⓐ ⓑ ⓒ ⓓ		

MS Windows 10

MCQs 1 Mark Questions

1. Which of the following acts as a interface between computer hardware and user?
   (a) Software (b) Operating system
   (c) Printer (d) Device drivers

2. .... is the most commonly used operating system in computers all over the world.
   (a) Linux (b) Mac
   (c) Ubuntu (d) Windows

3. Windows operating system is based on which of the following?
   (a) CUI (b) CGI
   (c) GUI (d) GLI

4. Windows 10 is the final version of windows which supports .... processors and devices with .... firmware.
   (a) 32-bit, BIOS
   (b) 64-bit, OS
   (c) 128-bit, Command line
   (d) 32-bit, OS

5. Windows 10 belongs to which family of windows?
   (a) Windows 7X (b) Windows NT
   (c) Windows NET (d) Windows XP

6. The Windows Runtime app ecosystem was revised into the .... in Windows 2010.
   (a) BIOS
   (b) Universal Windows Platform (UWP)
   (c) Task View
   (d) Cortana

7. Which of the following is a new default browser in Windows in place of Internet Explorer?
   (a) Microsoft Explorer
   (b) Microsoft Edge
   (c) Windows Edge
   (d) Google Chrome

8. If your computer has a touch screen then, you can go into .... mode anytime while working with Windows 2010.
   (a) Flight (b) Tablet
   (c) Desktop (d) Touchscreen

9. Which of the following features helps you to access frequently used settings and provides new notifications?
   (a) Windows Media Player
   (b) Microsoft Meet
   (c) Windows Action Centre
   (d) VLC

10. What is Xbox?

(a) A gaming console app
(b) A media player
(c) An audio channel
(d) Painting software

11. Which of the following features allows Windows 10 to adapt to different devices?

(a) Unifi (b) Continuum
(c) Flexi (d) Hub

12. .... is when the more power-hungry components, such as the monitor and the hard drive are put in idle for only a short time.

(a) Hibernation
(b) Power down
(c) Standby mode
(d) The shutdown procedure

13. The contents of .... are automatically cleared when you shut down your Windows operating system.

(a) ROM
(b) Cache
(c) RAM
(d) CD-ROM

14. Look at the given image and identify what it is in reference to Windows 2010?

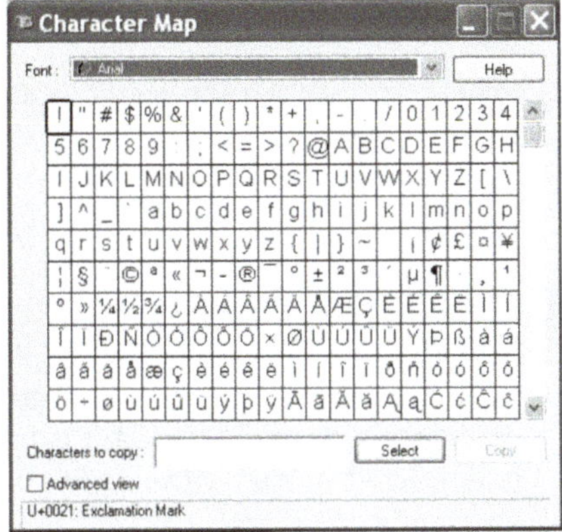

(a) Cortana (b) Character Map
(c) Accessories (d) Font Selection

15. Find the odd one out.

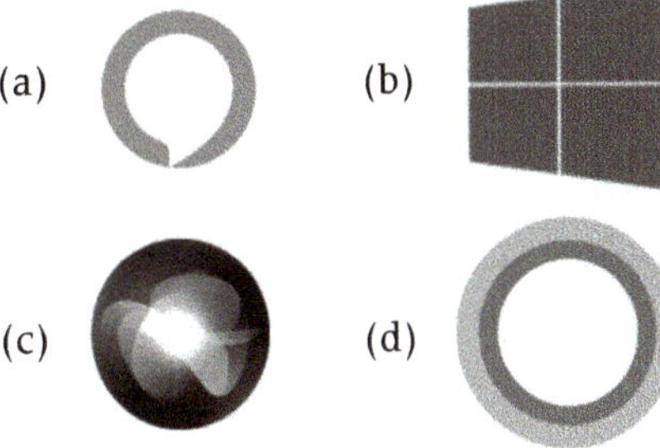

16. In Windows 10, when you click .... from the Start button, it reboots the computer and saves all the information on the hard drive.

It turns off the computer for a moment and then turns it back on again.

(a) Shut down (b) Hibernate
(c) Restart (d) Switch user

17. Seema wants to make a list of grocery items, set a reminder for her friend's birthday and update her schedule. In short, she needs an assistant. Which feature of Windows 10 will be able to accomplish all these tasks for her?

(a) Start menu (b) Google assistant
(c) Action centre (d) Cortana

18. A computer process that brings all the parts of a file together by moving the data blocks on a hard drive is known as

(a) drive compression
(b) drive backup
(c) disk backup
(d) disk defragmentation

19. The given key shortcut opens which pane in Windows?

(a) Navigation Pane
(b) Menu Pane
(c) Address Bar
(d) Task View Pane

20. In Windows, Icons such as Add/Remove program, Add New Hardware, Modems, etc, are found in

(a) Control Panel
(b) Network Neighbourhood
(c) My Computer
(d) Task Bar

21. If we wish to change the speed of the mouse we, are using then which of the following will help us in doing so?

(a) Taskbar
(b) Devices and Printers
(c) Navigation Panel
(d) Start

22. Swati wants to add different clocks to her system according to different time zones. How can she do so?

(a) Control panel → Clock → Language and Region → Date and time → Add clock for different time zones
(b) Control panel → Date and time → Clock, Language and Region → Add clock for different time zones
(c) Control panel → Clock, Language and Region → Add clock for different time zones
(d) Clock → Language and Region → Date and time → Add clock

23. What does the given screen image show in Windows?

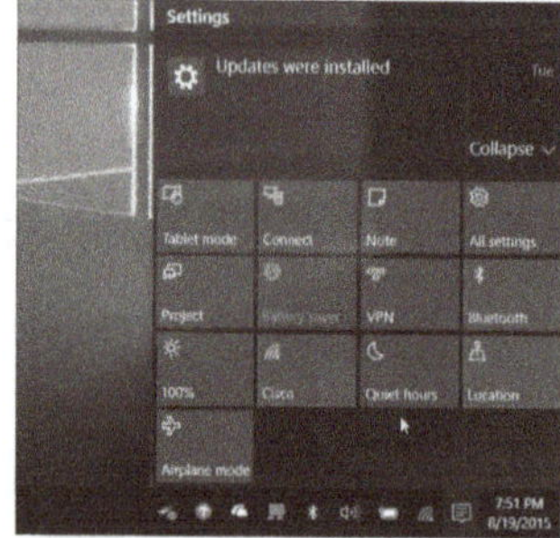

(a) Settings option
(b) Power options
(c) Troubleshoot options
(d) Screensaver

24. What does the given icon depict?

(a) Security option in Control Panel
(b) Hardware and Sound option in Control Panel
(c) Action Centre in Control Panel
(d) Network and Internet settings in Control Panel

25. What is the start menu?

(a) It provides a central launching point for computer programs and performing other tasks.
(b) It provides a point to delete programs on your computer.
(c) It does nothing.
(d) It provides the code for programs running in the background on the computer

26. What is the Quick Launch toolbar on Taskbar?

(a) It displays the time, clock and calendar on taskbar.
(b) It is used to open Windows and start new applications.
(c) It is a section of taskbar that enables the user to launch their programs without having to locate them using start menu.
(d) It displays sleep, hibernate options on the taskbar.

27. Where are the hidden icons located on the task bar?

(a) Top Left
(b) Top Right
(c) Bottom Left
(d) Bottom Right

MCQs 2 Mark Questions

28. Back up refers to a copy of computer disk/data that can be used if original one is damaged or lost. How can you take a backup in Windows 2010?

(a) In the search box on the taskbar, type restore files and then select Restore your files with file history.

(b) Select Start > Settings > Update and Security > Backup > Add a drive and then choose an external drive or network location for your backups.

(c) In the search box on the taskbar, type control panel. Then select Control Panel > System and Security > Backup and Restore.

(d) Select Start > Update and Security > Backup > Add a drive and then choose an external drive or network location for your backups.

29. Identify the tool with the help of given statements.

I. It allows users to minimise the unwanted open window applications on the screen.

II. To use it, we have to select or click upon the open window we are working on and shake it bi-directionally.

(a) Aero Peek (b) Aero Shake
(c) Xbox (d) Aero Snap

30. Which of the following statements is correct about My Lockbox?

I. It is an application to hide, lock files and applications run by users on Windows 10 and is one of the best feature of Windows 10.

II. It can help you in establishing some exceptional rules regarding execution of certain files and programs.

Codes

(a) Only I
(b) Only II
(c) Both I and II
(d) Neither I nor II

31. Read the given statements carefully and answer the question that follows.

I. It is a Windows Start mode which is useful when certain programs do not start correctly and need trouble shooting.

II. This mode starts windows with a limited set of drivers and files.

Which Start mode is being talked about in the above statements ?

(a) Troubleshooting
(b) Safe mode
(c) Auto mode
(d) Start mode

32. Identify the incorrect steps about showing Cortana in the taskbar.

I. Left click the taskbar → Click on toolbars

II. Left click the taskbar → Click on show Cortana button

III. Right click the taskbar → Click on show Cortana button

IV. Control panel → Show Cortana button

Codes

(a) I, II and III (b) II, III and IV
(c) I, II and IV (d) I, III and IV

Darken your choice with HB Pencil

1.	a b c d	7.	a b c d	13.	a b c d	19.	a b c d	25.	a b c d	31.	a b c d
2.	a b c d	8.	a b c d	14.	a b c d	20.	a b c d	26.	a b c d	32.	a b c d
3.	a b c d	9.	a b c d	15.	a b c d	21.	a b c d	27.	a b c d		
4.	a b c d	10.	a b c d	16.	a b c d	22.	a b c d	28.	a b c d		
5.	a b c d	11.	a b c d	17.	a b c d	23.	a b c d	29.	a b c d		
6.	a b c d	12.	a b c d	18.	a b c d	24.	a b c d	30.	a b c d		

MS Word 2016

MCQs 1 Mark Questions

1. .... is one of the primary utility feature of the Microsoft Office Package which helps us to create and edit personal and business documents, letters, etc.
   (a) MS Excel (b) MS PowerPoint
   (c) MS Word (d) MS Office

2. MS Word is supported on both .... and .... platforms.
   (a) Windows, Mac
   (b) BIOS, Mac
   (c) Tablet, BIOS
   (d) BIOS, PC

3. You can choose a template, a new document or access recent documents with the help of which of the following?
   (a) Start screen
   (b) Screen saver
   (c) Export
   (d) Print screen

4. The Save, Undo and Redo commands are available in
   (a) Menu bar
   (b) Style bar
   (c) Quick Access Toolbar
   (d) Taskbar

5. Which of the following options allows you to adjust alignment and spacing in a document?
   (a) Ribbon (b) Ruler
   (c) Zoom (d) Scroll bar

6. Which of the following allows you to search for commands especially if you can't find a specific command?
   (a) Quick Access Toolbar
   (b) Start Screen
   (c) Ruler
   (d) Tell Me Bar

7. .... has multiple tabs, each with several groups of commands to perform common tasks in Word.
   (a) Ribbon (b) Page layout
   (c) Alignments (d) References

8. What are the different modes in which a document can be viewed in Word?
   (a) Print layout, Macros, Mailings
   (b) Read mode, Print layout, Web layout
   (c) Read mode, Zoom control, Thumbnails
   (d) Web layout, Print layout, Auto read

9. Which of the following is a default extension in Word files?
   (a) .pdf (b) .wrd
   (c) .doc (d) .docx

10. You can .... a document to remove personal info and .... it to prevent others from making changes to it using the Information pane.

(a) protect, inspect (b) safe, protect
(c) inspect, protect (d) prevent, block

11. Identify the function of the given icon.

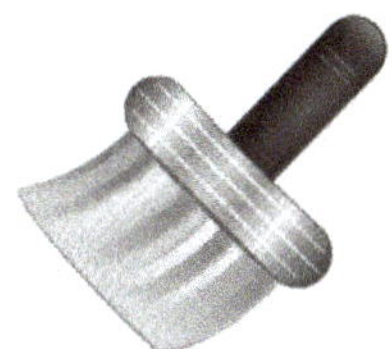

(a) It is used to fill color in the text.
(b) It is used to quickly apply same formatting such as color, font style and size or border style to multiple pieces of text or graphics.
(c) It is used to copy text from one place to another.
(d) It is used to erase the contents of a document.

12. Look at the given image. What is this technique of inserting ghost text or images in a document called ?

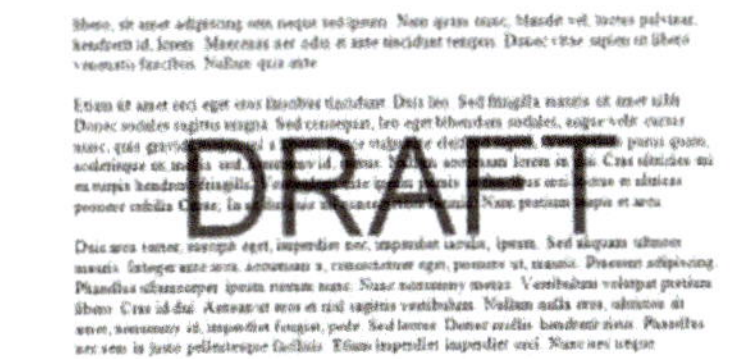

(a) Ghosting (b) Highlighting
(c) Watermark (d) Paint

13. What is the function of the given feature in Word?

(a) Spelling and grammar check
(b) Thesaurus
(c) Research
(d) Translate

14. Identify the feature which arranges all the windows in Word.

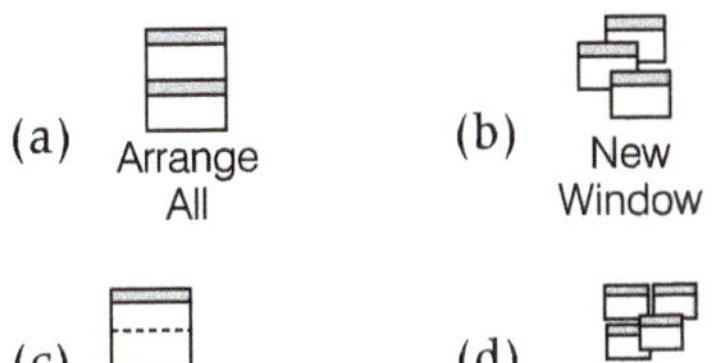

15. What do the following icons signify ?

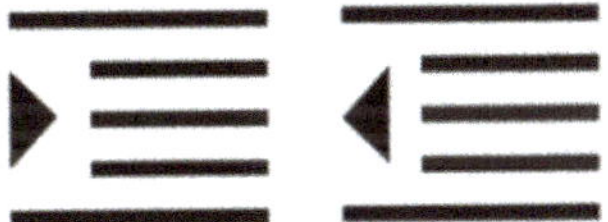

(a) Align left and right
(b) Indent left and right
(c) Increase and decrease indent
(d) Decrease and increase indent

16. Swati wants to change the look of her Word document. Look at the image given below and choose the correct sequence of steps to help Swati.

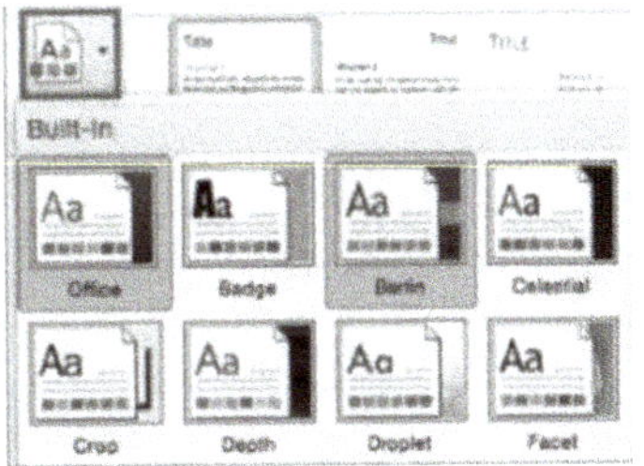

(a) Page layout → Themes
(b) Insert → Themes
(c) Page layout → Orientation
(d) Home → Change styles

17. What is the use of the selected icon in the given image in a Word document?

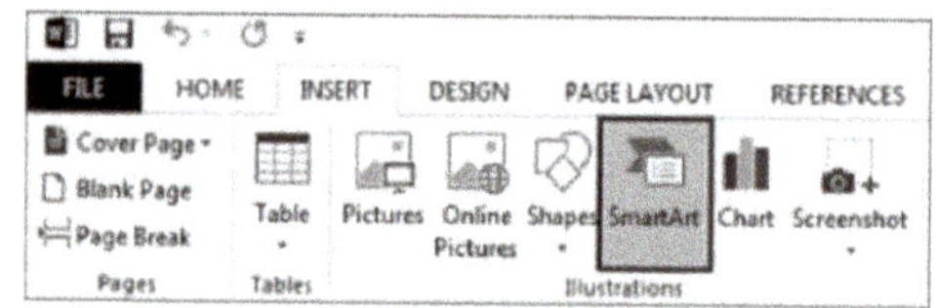

(a) To visually communicate information with graphics instead of just using text
(b) To insert images in a document
(c) To insert shapes in a document
(d) To insert charts, tables in a document

18. What do the following icons depict about formatting a paragraph?

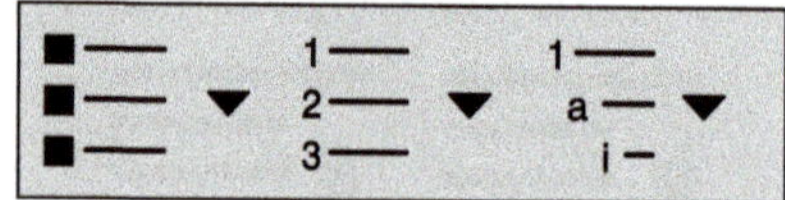

(a) Text alignment
(b) Font styles
(c) Bullets, Numbering and Multilevel list
(d) Line spacing and indentation

19. .... and .... can be inserted using the following icons.

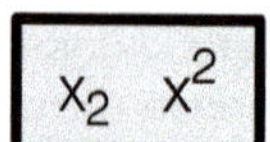

(a) Bold, Italics
(b) Subscript, Superscript
(c) Capital, Small
(d) Text highlight, Font color

20. What do the following images represent in Word?

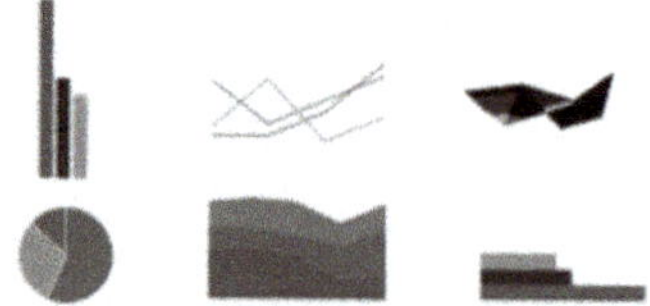

(a) Types of Tables
(b) Types of Charts
(c) Types of Clip Art
(d) Types of Shapes

21. .... is used to generate a special line of text for each mail recipient.
(a) Recipients
(b) Greeting line
(c) Address block
(d) Rules

22. What do the following icons depict in the Mailings tab of Word?

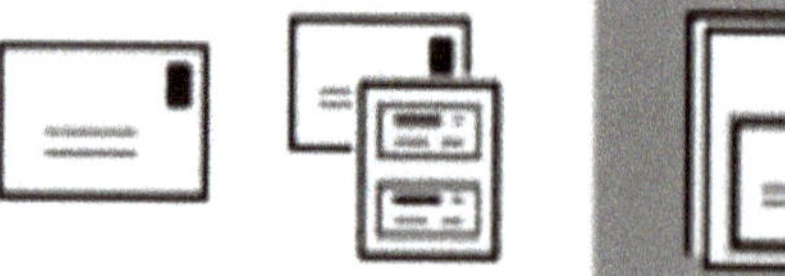

(a) Mail Merge, Labels, Envelope
(b) Envelope, Labels, Start, Mail Merge
(c) Select recipients, Address block, Greeting line
(d) Highlight Merge field, Preview, Recipients

23. Which of the following tabs has the following features as shown in the image?

(a) New comment in Review
(b) Track changes in Review
(c) Table of contents in Reference
(d) Select recipients in Mail Merge

MCQs 2 Mark Questions

24. Which of the following is correct about Gutter margin?

(a) Margin that is added to the left margin when printing.

(b) Margin that is added to the right margin when printing.

(c) Margin that is added to the binding side of page when printing.

(d) Margin that is added to the outside of the page when printing.

25. Which statement is true about Drop Cap in MS Word ?

I. It is a large capital letter used as a decorative element at the beginning of a paragraph or section.

II. To insert Drop cap, Click anywhere in the paragraph you want to change.

Codes

(a) Only I

(b) Only II

(c) Both I and II

(d) Neither I nor II

26. Identify the command based on the given statements.

I. It can be inserted using the Layout tab in word and shows the line number where cursor is currently positioned.

II. It appears to the left of each line on a page, and Word allows you to control the distance between it and the text of the document.

Codes

(a) Page number

(b) Line number

(c) Document number

(d) Header

Directions (Q. Nos. 27 and 28) *Look at the given chart and answer the following questions.*

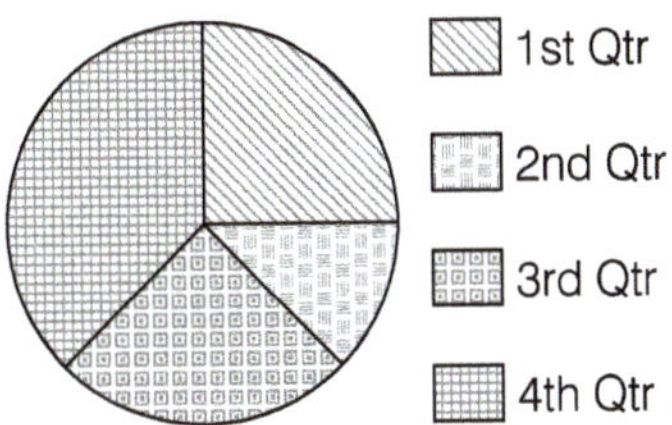

27. How can you convert the given chart to a different type?

(a) Click the Chart area → On Design tab in type group click change chart type

Or Select Chart area → Chart design tab → Type group → Change chart type

(b) Select Chart→ Chart tools → Layout → 3D Tools

(c) Select Chart → Design → Chart layout → Quick layout

(d) Select Chart → Chart Tools → Design → Select Data

28. What are the given values called?

(a) Chart title (b) Trend line

(c) Axis title (d) Legends

29. Which of the following statements is/are correct about Mailings?

I. This tab contains all the mailing options and also the font and position/alignment of the addresses.

II. The Mailings tab has five groups of related commands; Create, Start Mail Merge, Write and Insert Fields, Preview Results and Finish.

Codes

(a) Only I

(b) Only II

(c) Both the I and II

(d) Neither I nor II

30. Match the following lists.

List I (Key Shortcut)	List II (Functions)
A. Ctrl + N	1. Move to the next cell in MS Word
B. Shift + Home	2. Selects a sentence
C. 3 Time Pressing F8	3. Shortcut used to create new document
D. Alt + F + A	4. Select rows from left to right
E. Tab	5. Opening dialog box

Codes

	A	B	C	D	E
(a)	1	3	2	4	5
(b)	5	1	4	3	2
(c)	3	4	2	5	1
(d)	5	2	3	4	1

31. Which of the following is incorrectly matched?

	Icons	Functions
(a)		Paragraph alignment options
(b)		Insert rows & columns
(c)		Window arrangement options
(d)		Page border options

Darken your choice with HB Pencil

1.	ⓐ ⓑ ⓒ ⓓ	7.	ⓐ ⓑ ⓒ ⓓ	13.	ⓐ ⓑ ⓒ ⓓ	19.	ⓐ ⓑ ⓒ ⓓ	25.	ⓐ ⓑ ⓒ ⓓ	31.	ⓐ ⓑ ⓒ ⓓ
2.	ⓐ ⓑ ⓒ ⓓ	8.	ⓐ ⓑ ⓒ ⓓ	14.	ⓐ ⓑ ⓒ ⓓ	20.	ⓐ ⓑ ⓒ ⓓ	26.	ⓐ ⓑ ⓒ ⓓ		
3.	ⓐ ⓑ ⓒ ⓓ	9.	ⓐ ⓑ ⓒ ⓓ	15.	ⓐ ⓑ ⓒ ⓓ	21.	ⓐ ⓑ ⓒ ⓓ	27.	ⓐ ⓑ ⓒ ⓓ		
4.	ⓐ ⓑ ⓒ ⓓ	10.	ⓐ ⓑ ⓒ ⓓ	16.	ⓐ ⓑ ⓒ ⓓ	22.	ⓐ ⓑ ⓒ ⓓ	28.	ⓐ ⓑ ⓒ ⓓ		
5.	ⓐ ⓑ ⓒ ⓓ	11.	ⓐ ⓑ ⓒ ⓓ	17.	ⓐ ⓑ ⓒ ⓓ	23.	ⓐ ⓑ ⓒ ⓓ	29.	ⓐ ⓑ ⓒ ⓓ		
6.	ⓐ ⓑ ⓒ ⓓ	12.	ⓐ ⓑ ⓒ ⓓ	18.	ⓐ ⓑ ⓒ ⓓ	24.	ⓐ ⓑ ⓒ ⓓ	30.	ⓐ ⓑ ⓒ ⓓ		

MS Excel 2016

MCQs 1 Mark Questions

1. .... is an electronic spreadsheet with numerous rows and columns, used for organising data, graphically represent data and performing different calculations.
   (a) MS Excel (b) MS Word
   (c) MS PowerPoint (d) MS Office

2. MS Excel is a part of .... suite.
   (a) MS Excel (b) MS Word
   (c) MS PowerPoint (d) MS Office

3. A row and column together make a .... in MS Excel.
   (a) worksheet (b) cell
   (c) result (d) spreadsheet

4. The address or name of a cell or a range of cells is known as
   (a) Cell value (b) Cell ID
   (c) Cell reference (d) All of these

5. What is the file made of rows and columns in Excel called which helps in sorting, organising and arranging data efficiently?
   (a) Cell (b) Row
   (c) Column (d) Spreadsheet

6. By default, Excel has .... Spreadsheets.
   (a) one (b) two
   (c) three (d) four

7. What is the collection of Spreadsheets in Excel called?
   (a) Worksheet (b) Workbook
   (c) File (d) Data

8. What is the function of the given icon in Excel?

   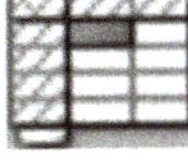

   (a) New Window
   (b) Split cells
   (c) Freeze panes
   (d) Duplicate cells

9. What is the function of the given icon?

   (a) To save workspace
   (b) To insert functions
   (c) To insert symbols
   (d) To create new worksheet

10. How can you open a new worksheet in Excel?

(a) Right click on the tab of existing worksheet → Click insert

(b) Select the worksheet → On Home tab → Cells group → Click insert → Click insert sheet

(c) Select existing worksheet → Press shift + F11

(d) All of the above

11. What do the following icons signify?

(a) Insert, Delete and Format cells only

(b) Insert, Delete and Format cells and worksheet both

(c) Insert symbols and formula

(d) Conditional formatting

12. How can you wrap text in a cell?

(a) Select cell → Home → Wrap text

(b) Select cell → Alignment → Wrap text

(c) Select cell → Home tab → Alignment group → Wrap text

(d) Select cell → Home → Alignment → Merge and center

13. Which component of Excel window allows you to type formula?

(a) Toolbar (b) Formula tab

(c) Calculation bar (d) Insert bar

14. What is the extension of a MS Excel file?

(a) .exl (b) .xl (c) .xlsx (d) excl

15. Shyam wants to navigate between different worksheets. Which of the given shortcuts will he use?

(a) Shift + Pg Up

(b) Alt + Pg Down

(c) Click on the desired sheet

(d) Ctrl + Pg Up

16. What are the steps to insert a new row in a worksheet?

(a) Edit → New Row

(b) File → New Row

(c) Format → Row

(d) Home → tab → Cells group → Insert → Insert Sheet Rows

17. How can you add different functions like Math, logical functions, Date and Time etc., to your worksheet?

(a) Calculation tab

(b) Function library

(c) Page setup

(d) Sheet options

18. What combination of keys will help you select the entire row of the active cell?

(a) Ctrl + F1

(b) Alt + Space bar

(c) Ctrl + Space bar

(d) Shift + Space bar

19. .... is the process of combining selected cells into one cell.

(a) Sorting (b) Merging

(c) Aligning (d) Moving

20. How can you add name to your worksheet?

(a) Formulas tab Defined Names group-Define Name

(b) Formulas-Defined Names Tab-Name number

(c) Formulas-Defined Names Tab-Name Manager

(d) Formulas- Name number

21. A .... is an interactive way to quickly summarise large amounts of data.

(a) Pivot Table (b) Formula

(c) Refresh all (d) Sort

22. .... will remove duplicates, keep the first record of the duplicate records and provide a summary of the number of rows that have been removed.

(a)

(b) 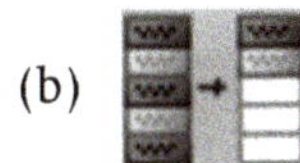

(c) 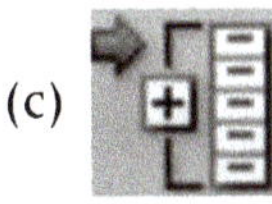

(d) 

23. Which of the following statements is not true?
    (a) Cell contents of MS Excel can be modified using edit commands.
    (b) Cancel and enter buttons are found on formula bar.
    (c) When you double click the cell, it allows you to perform minor changes.
    (d) In MS Excel, calculations can only be performed using formula.

MCQs 2 Mark Questions

24. Which of the following statements explains the function of the given icon correctly?

I. It is used to automatically create a formula to sum all the numbers in a continuous range.
II. Average, Min., Max. etc. are all a part of this function.

Codes
(a) Only I
(b) Only II
(c) Both the I and II
(d) Neither I nor II

25. In a school, the marks details of class-VI students are entered in an Excel sheet. What is/are the quickest way to access the details of a particular student in the worksheet?

I. The details of a particular student can be accessed by typing the name of the student in the name box.
II. The details of a particular student can be accessed by typing the name of the student in the font box.

Codes
(a) Only I
(b) Only II
(c) Both the I and II
(d) Neither I nor II

26. Which of the following is the correct sequence of adding image to the background of an Excel sheet?
    (a) Select Current sheet → Page layout tab → Page Setup group → Background
    (b) Current sheet → Page Layout → Print titles
    (c) Current sheet → Insert → Background
    (d) Current sheet →View → Background view

27. Identify the incorrect statements from the following.

I. You can protect a worksheet as well as a workbook by choosing the respective options from the Review tab.
II. It is not possible in Excel to protect worksheet as well as a workbook.

Codes
(a) Only I
(b) Both the I and II
(c) Neither I nor II
(d) Only II

28. Which of the following statements correctly describes the function of Selection Pane in Excel?

I. It is where data or formulas entered into a worksheet appear for the active cell.

II. It lets you manage all the objects on your worksheet.

Codes

(a) Only I
(b) Both the I and II
(c) Neither I nor II
(d) Only II

29. Match the following lists.

List I (Key Shortcut)	List II (Function)
A. Ctrl + C, Ctrl + V	1. To hide selected row
B. Ctrl + 9	2. To open the Data tab
C. Ctrl + Shift + 9	3. To copy and paste cells
D. Alt + A	4. To unhide any hidden rows

Codes

	A	B	C	D
(a)	3	1	4	2
(b)	1	2	3	4
(c)	2	3	4	1
(d)	1	4	3	2

30. Match the following lists.

List I (Icon)	List II (Function)
A. Ω	1. To insert different types of Charts
B. fx	2. Workbook views
C. [workbook view icons]	3. To insert symbol
D. [chart icons]	4. To insert any function

Codes

	A	B	C	D
(a)	2	1	4	3
(b)	3	1	4	2
(c)	3	4	2	1
(d)	4	3	2	1

Darken your choice with HB Pencil

1. ⓐ ⓑ ⓒ ⓓ	6. ⓐ ⓑ ⓒ ⓓ	11. ⓐ ⓑ ⓒ ⓓ	16. ⓐ ⓑ ⓒ ⓓ	21. ⓐ ⓑ ⓒ ⓓ	26. ⓐ ⓑ ⓒ ⓓ
2. ⓐ ⓑ ⓒ ⓓ	7. ⓐ ⓑ ⓒ ⓓ	12. ⓐ ⓑ ⓒ ⓓ	17. ⓐ ⓑ ⓒ ⓓ	22. ⓐ ⓑ ⓒ ⓓ	27. ⓐ ⓑ ⓒ ⓓ
3. ⓐ ⓑ ⓒ ⓓ	8. ⓐ ⓑ ⓒ ⓓ	13. ⓐ ⓑ ⓒ ⓓ	18. ⓐ ⓑ ⓒ ⓓ	23. ⓐ ⓑ ⓒ ⓓ	28. ⓐ ⓑ ⓒ ⓓ
4. ⓐ ⓑ ⓒ ⓓ	9. ⓐ ⓑ ⓒ ⓓ	14. ⓐ ⓑ ⓒ ⓓ	19. ⓐ ⓑ ⓒ ⓓ	24. ⓐ ⓑ ⓒ ⓓ	29. ⓐ ⓑ ⓒ ⓓ
5. ⓐ ⓑ ⓒ ⓓ	10. ⓐ ⓑ ⓒ ⓓ	15. ⓐ ⓑ ⓒ ⓓ	20. ⓐ ⓑ ⓒ ⓓ	25. ⓐ ⓑ ⓒ ⓓ	30. ⓐ ⓑ ⓒ ⓓ

MS PowerPoint 2016

MCQs 1 Mark Questions

1. .... is a software used to make presentations.
   (a) MS WORD
   (b) MS EXCEL
   (c) MS PowerPoint
   (d) MS OFFICE

2. The pages in a presentation are known as
   (a) documents (b) slides
   (c) sheets (d) workbooks

3. Which of the following is an incorrect sequence of steps to open MS PowerPoint?
   (a) → MS PowerPoint 2016
   (b) → All programs → MS PowerPoint 2016
   (c) →Search bar → MS PowerPoint 2016-Enter
   (d) → All programs → Windows Presentation Maker

4. By which feature, you can choose different ways to display information on a slide?
   (a) Slide Show (b) Slide views
   (c) Slide Number (d) Slide Layout

5. What is the use of the given feature in PowerPoint?

   (a) Slide size scale (b) Slide view
   (c) Slide show (d) Slide arrange

6. What is the name of a pre-designed presentation which includes custom formatting and designs?
   (a) Layout (b) Theme
   (c) Template (d) Slide

7. What is the name of a tool that can be used to color shapes in PowerPoint ?
   (a) Shape Fill (b) Eyedropper
   (c) Notes (d) Put color

8. .... is a feature which changes the background of a slide.
   (a) Change styles
   (b) Slide orientation
   (c) Background styles
   (d) Insert style

9. The blank space below a slide is used for writing
   (a) Notes (b) Slide number
   (c) Slide title (d) Slide content

10. The following icons are used to insert .... and .... in a presentation.

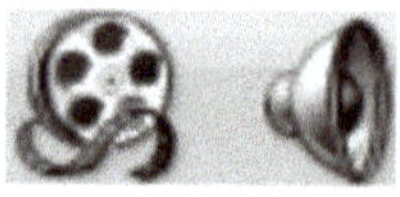

(a) Text, Graphics (b) Movie, Sound
(c) Sound, Movie (d) Image, Audio

11. Which bar shows the slide number, theme, language, zoom settings in a PowerPoint window?

(a) Title bar
(b) Tool bar
(c) Status bar
(d) Access Toolbar

12. What do these icons on a status bar of a PowerPoint window signify?

(a) Slide view, Slide Sorter view
(b) Normal view, Slide sorter view, Slide show view
(c) Normal view, Slide show view
(d) Slide layout view, Slide number view

13. What is the other name of Menu Bar?

(a) Status bar
(b) Title bar
(c) Toolkit
(d) Quick Access Toolbar

14. By default, a menu bar in PowerPoint has the following actions.

(a) Save, Undo, Redo, Office Button, Quick access, Toolbar
(b) Copy, Paste, Cut, Select
(c) Copy, Paste, Save, Undo
(d) Start from beginning, Select

15. A little arrow at the end of the Menu bar can be used to .... it.

(a) Format (b) Customise
(c) Delete (d) Remove

16. How can you create a new presentation in PowerPoint?

(a) Open PowerPoint → New → Blank presentation → Create
(b) Open PowerPoint → Press Ctrl+N
(c) Both (a) and (b)
(d) None of the above

17. How can you insert a new slide in your presentation?

(a) Home-Layout (b) Ctrl+M
(c) Both (a) and (b) (d) None of these

18. Choose the correct icon through which you can change the slide orientation in your presentation.

(a)  (b) 

(c) 

(d) 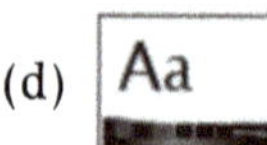

19. Which of the following options lets you add different themes and background styles to your presentation?

(a) Animation (b) Transition
(c) Design (d) Review

20. Dissolve, Newsflash, Shape circle, Shape diamond are all types of .... which can be inserted using the .... tab.

(a) Font styles, Home
(b) Transitions, Animation
(c) Movements, Animation
(d) Previews, Review

21. Which of the following will begin the slide show from current slide?

(a)  (b) 

(c)   

22. Shyam wanted to store the information about the theme and slide layouts (color, font, effects etc.) of his presentation. How can he do so?
(a) Insert Slide sorter
(b) Insert Slide Pane
(c) Insert Slide Master
(d) Insert Slide Number

23. You can swap(exchange slide positions) in your presentation using
(a) Slide Sorter (b) Handout
(c) Notes page (d) Notes Master

24. You can change the order of slides in your presentation using
(a) Outline Pane (b) Slides Pane
(c) Slide Shift (d) Slide Preview

25. Choose the Correct sequence of steps to insert new slide using Slides Pane.
(a) Left click on the Slides Pane-New slide
(b) Right click on the Slides Pane-New slide
(c) Right click on the Slides Pane-Cut
(d) Right click on the Slides Pane-Paste

26. There are three types of views in status bar in PowerPoint. Choose the correct ones from the options given below:
(a) Normal view, slide sorter view, Slide show view
(b) Normal view, notes view, Slide view
(c) Slide sorter view, Notes view, Presenter view
(d) Normal view, Presenter view, Slide view

27. Which of the following views allows you to present the slides similar to a slide show view but the PowerPoint Title Bar and Status Bar are also visible on the screen?
(a) Slide Sorter view
(b) Normal View
(c) Reading View
(d) Editing View

MCQs 2 Mark Questions

28. Shyam has converted the text in image (I) to a text in image (II) What is this feature called?

(a) Convert to Clip art
(b) Convert to Graphic art
(c) Convert to SmartArt
(d) Convert to Picture

29. What are the given two views of a PowerPoint window called?

I.

II.

(a) Slides, Outline
(b) Browse, Comments
(c) Slides, Comments
(d) Browse, Outline

30. Which of the following statements are correct about Notes page View in a Presentation?
I. Notes Page View allows you to view the Notes written at the bottom of each slide.

II. You can take a print out of the Notes Pages to use as reference while presenting the slides.

Codes

(a) Both I and II
(b) Only I
(c) Neither I nor II
(d) Only II

31. Which statement describes the function of Handouts Master correctly?

I. Handouts contain a summary of the presentation to make it easily understandable for the audience.

II. A handout contains thumbnails of slides and a few printed lines about each slide.

Codes

(a) Both I and II (b) Only I
(c) Neither I nor II (d) Only II

32. Identify the feature of a PowerPoint presentation by reading the given statements carefully.

I. You can record a narration for your presentation using this feature which means your audio can be played back along with the full screen slide show.

II. You can also set up & rehearse timings for your presentation using this feature.

(a) Set up slide show, Hide slide
(b) Record Narration, Rehearse timings
(c) Custom Slide Show, Rehearse timings
(d) Record Narration, Hide slide

33. Matching the following lists.

List I (Function)	**List II** (Key Shortcut)
A. Go to Insert tab	1. Alt+H
B. Open Home tab	2. Page down
C. Go to the next slide	3. Alt+N
D. Cut selected text, object or slide	4. Ctrl+X

Codes

	A	B	C	D		A	B	C	D
(a)	3	1	2	4	(b)	2	3	1	4
(c)	4	1	3	2	(d)	1	3	2	4

34. Which of the following pair is incorrectly matched

	Icon	**Function**
(a)	Click to add title / Click to add subtitle	Page layout
(b)		Protect Presentation
(c)		Apply transition to all slides
(d)		Format Painter

Darken your choice with HB Pencil

1.	ⓐ ⓑ ⓒ ⓓ	7.	ⓐ ⓑ ⓒ ⓓ	13.	ⓐ ⓑ ⓒ ⓓ	19.	ⓐ ⓑ ⓒ ⓓ	25.	ⓐ ⓑ ⓒ ⓓ	31.	ⓐ ⓑ ⓒ ⓓ
2.	ⓐ ⓑ ⓒ ⓓ	8.	ⓐ ⓑ ⓒ ⓓ	14.	ⓐ ⓑ ⓒ ⓓ	20.	ⓐ ⓑ ⓒ ⓓ	26.	ⓐ ⓑ ⓒ ⓓ	32.	ⓐ ⓑ ⓒ ⓓ
3.	ⓐ ⓑ ⓒ ⓓ	9.	ⓐ ⓑ ⓒ ⓓ	15.	ⓐ ⓑ ⓒ ⓓ	21.	ⓐ ⓑ ⓒ ⓓ	27.	ⓐ ⓑ ⓒ ⓓ	33.	ⓐ ⓑ ⓒ ⓓ
4.	ⓐ ⓑ ⓒ ⓓ	10.	ⓐ ⓑ ⓒ ⓓ	16.	ⓐ ⓑ ⓒ ⓓ	22.	ⓐ ⓑ ⓒ ⓓ	28.	ⓐ ⓑ ⓒ ⓓ	34.	ⓐ ⓑ ⓒ ⓓ
5.	ⓐ ⓑ ⓒ ⓓ	11.	ⓐ ⓑ ⓒ ⓓ	17.	ⓐ ⓑ ⓒ ⓓ	23.	ⓐ ⓑ ⓒ ⓓ	29.	ⓐ ⓑ ⓒ ⓓ		
6.	ⓐ ⓑ ⓒ ⓓ	12.	ⓐ ⓑ ⓒ ⓓ	18.	ⓐ ⓑ ⓒ ⓓ	24.	ⓐ ⓑ ⓒ ⓓ	30.	ⓐ ⓑ ⓒ ⓓ		

Introduction to QBASIC

MCQs 1 Mark Questions

1. .... is a high-level programming language developed by .... in 1991.
   (a) Quicker basics, Microsoft
   (b) QBASIC, Microsoft
   (c) Quickbasic, IBM
   (d) QBASIC, IBM

2. QBASIC is based on which of the following operating systems ?
   (a) Mac
   (b) Unix
   (c) Command prompt
   (d) DOS

3. In QBASIC, ... is used to gather information from a user.
   (a) Input (b) Output
   (c) Program (d) Commands

4. The source code(program) in QBASIC can only be immediately executed by the built-in
   (a) Compiler
   (b) Command prompt
   (c) Interpreter
   (d) Assembler

5. Which of the following constructs are possible in QBASIC?
   (a) Sequential (b) Decision making
   (c) Loops (d) All of these

6. Which of the following features is present in Quick basic but absent in QBASIC?
   (a) Compiler (b) Executable files
   (c) Both(a) and (b) (d) None of these

7. Quick basic has .... number of commands than QBASIC.
   (a) more (b) less
   (c) complicated (d) simple

8. The QBASIC window contains which of the following components?
   (a) Status bar (b) Menu bar
   (c) Program title (d) All of these

9. Which of the following shows the shortcut keys and location of cursor on screen?
   (a) Menu bar (b) Status bar
   (c) Program mode (d) Shortcut view

10. In which of the following modes, the commands are executed immediately and are stored in computer's memory?
    (a) Editor Immediate Mode
    (b) Power Saving Mode
    (c) Editor Program Mode
    (d) Performance Mode

11. Which of the following comes under the Character set of QBASIC?
    (a) Small and capital alphabets
    (b) 0 to 9 numbers
    (c) Special characters
    (d) All of the above

12. The words in QBASIC which have a special meaning are called

(a) program (b) commands
(c) instructions (d) keywords

13. Name $ is a way of writing a

(a) Numeric variable
(b) String variable
(c) Constant
(d) Loop

14. Which of the following is an incorrect numeric variable?

(a) people (b) programming12
(c) seven11 (d) @basiccode#

15. Which of the following are examples of String constant?

(a) "Delhi"
(b) "Meerut"
(c) Both (a) and (b)
(d) Seema123

16. Which of the following are used to compare two values of same type?

(a) Arithmetic operators
(b) Logical operators
(c) Numeric constants
(d) Relational operators

17. .... is the combination of operators, constants and variables that is evaluated to get a result.

(a) Expression (b) Input
(c) Output (d) String

18. Which of the following sets the position of the next character to be shown on screen or printed on paper?

(a) WRITE (b) INPUT
(c) PRINT (d) TAB

19. .... command is used to clear the screen in QBASIC.

(a) DELETE (b) SELECT
(c) PRINT (d) CLS

20. Which operation will be performed if the expression is 3^3 and the result is 27?

(a) Division (b) Multiplication
(c) Addition (d) Exponential

21. Which of the following statements is used to assign a value or a number to a variable?

(a) IF (b) LET
(c) LOOP (d) GOTO

22. .... is a process in which a part of a program can be executed repeatedly in QBASIC.

(a) Grouping (b) Compiling
(c) Looping (d) Assigning

23. What do you understand by the given statement

A<=B

(a) B is less or equal to A
(b) B is equal to A
(c) A is less or equal to B
(d) A is equal to B

24. Which operation would be performed first in the given expression?

A*B – C+D^E/F

(a) A*B (b) B – C
(c) D^E (d) E/F

MCQs 2 Mark Questions

25. What will come in the place of '?' in the following table?

String Data (A$)
String Data (B$)
A$+B$
"Seema"
"Deepak"
?
12
22
?

(a) Seema,12 (b) Deepak,22
(c) 1222 (d) SeemaDeepak 1222

26. Which of the following statements is correct about Qbasic?

I. In Qbasic,'?' can be used in place of PRINT command.

II. Each and every program in Qbasic should begin with SET command and end with 'TERMINATE' command.

Codes

(a) Only I (b) Both I and II

(c) Only II (d) Neither I nor II

27. Which of the following pair is incorrect?

	Quickbasic	Qbasic
I.	It is a commercial software.	It is a trial based software.
II.	It has limited storage and number of functions.	It has large storage and offers different functions.

Codes

(a) Only I

(b) Both I and II

(c) Only II

(d) Neither I nor II

28. What will be the output of the given program?

```
CLS
LET A$=HELLO
LET S$=HOW
LET D$=ARE
LET F$=YOU
PRINT A$;D$;F$
```

(a) HELLO HOW ARE YOU

(b) HOW ARE YOU

(c) HELLO HOW ARE

(d) HELLO ARE YOU

Darken your choice with HB Pencil

1.	ⓐ ⓑ ⓒ ⓓ	6.	ⓐ ⓑ ⓒ ⓓ	11.	ⓐ ⓑ ⓒ ⓓ	16.	ⓐ ⓑ ⓒ ⓓ	21.	ⓐ ⓑ ⓒ ⓓ	26.	ⓐ ⓑ ⓒ ⓓ
2.	ⓐ ⓑ ⓒ ⓓ	7.	ⓐ ⓑ ⓒ ⓓ	12.	ⓐ ⓑ ⓒ ⓓ	17.	ⓐ ⓑ ⓒ ⓓ	22.	ⓐ ⓑ ⓒ ⓓ	27.	ⓐ ⓑ ⓒ ⓓ
3.	ⓐ ⓑ ⓒ ⓓ	8.	ⓐ ⓑ ⓒ ⓓ	13.	ⓐ ⓑ ⓒ ⓓ	18.	ⓐ ⓑ ⓒ ⓓ	23.	ⓐ ⓑ ⓒ ⓓ	28.	ⓐ ⓑ ⓒ ⓓ
4.	ⓐ ⓑ ⓒ ⓓ	9.	ⓐ ⓑ ⓒ ⓓ	14.	ⓐ ⓑ ⓒ ⓓ	19.	ⓐ ⓑ ⓒ ⓓ	24.	ⓐ ⓑ ⓒ ⓓ		
5.	ⓐ ⓑ ⓒ ⓓ	10.	ⓐ ⓑ ⓒ ⓓ	15.	ⓐ ⓑ ⓒ ⓓ	20.	ⓐ ⓑ ⓒ ⓓ	25.	ⓐ ⓑ ⓒ ⓓ		

Internet and Email

MCQs 1 Mark Questions

1. .... is a world-wide global system of inter-connected computers.
   (a) Intranet (b) Supernet
   (c) Internet (d) Arpanet

2. Which of the following is a unique set of numbers which identifies a computer location on Internet or a local network?
   (a) DNS (b) IP address
   (c) Internet protocol (d) Website

3. The full form of DNS is .... It translates human readable domain names to Machine readable IP addresses.
   (a) Do not serve
   (b) Daily Network Service
   (c) Domain Name System
   (d) Domain Name Server

4. The .... is one of the biggest services of Internet which is used by billions of people.
   (a) World Wide Web
   (b) Google
   (c) Website
   (d) Network

5. From which of the following concepts, was the Internet developed?
   (a) IRPANET (b) ARPANET
   (c) ARNAPET (d) INTRANET

6. The Internet was developed in .... but for general public, its services began in ....
   (a) 1960, 1990 (b) 1990, 1960
   (c) 1960, 2000 (d) 1990, 2003

7. Which of the following is a device which connects one computer to another through a telephone line?
   (a) Dial-up (b) Modem
   (c) Broadband (d) Web Browser

8. The companies that provide Internet are called
   (a) Internet Service Provider
   (b) Internet Facility Provider
   (c) Internet Availability Provider
   (d) Website

9. Identify the type of Internet connection in the given picture.

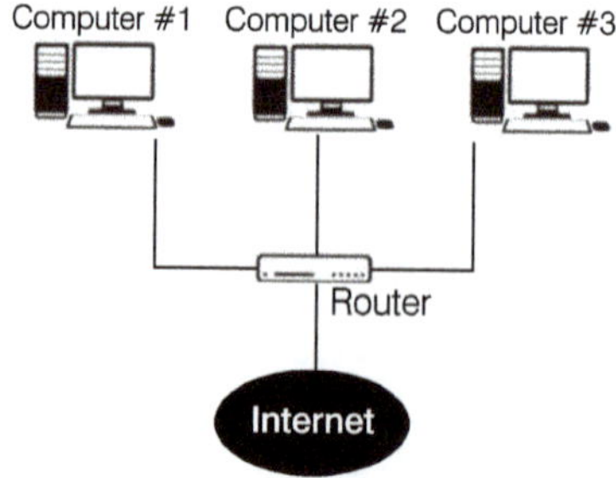

   (a) Dial-up (b) Cable
   (c) Satellite (d) Broadband

10. DSL, ADSL, SDSL all require .... to transmit data.
(a) Router (b) Telephone lines
(c) Satellite (d) Cellphone

11. Nowadays, ... cables are used for faster transmission of data. They transfer data in the form of light waves through thin glass threads.
(a) Wired
(b) Twisted
(c) Optical fibre
(d) Digital fibre

12. Which type of Internet connection is best for providing telecommunication services to a large number of people?
(a) Satellite (b) Dial-up
(c) Broadband (d) Cellular

13. To connect to the Internet from your computer, choose from the available list of networks, enter the .... and click on ....
(a) Password, disconnect
(b) Security key, connect
(c) Captcha, connect
(d) login, disconnect

14. The .... protocol is the main communication protocol which establishes an Internet connection and allows internetworking.
(a) Media (b) Online
(c) Internet (d) Open system

15. Which of the following is the standard Internet protocol?
(a) FTP (b) TCP/IP
(c) HTTP (d) NTTP

16. Which of the following protocols provides a standard communication network for web browsers and servers?
(a) NTTP (b) FTP
(c) PTP (d) HTTP

17. A .... is an application software that is used to access the World Wide Web.
(a) Web browser
(b) Search engine
(c) Website
(d) HTML

18. What is the other name of a collection of Web pages?
(a) URL (b) IP address
(c) Website (d) Home page

19. .... is used to create web pages.
(a) HTTP (b) Google
(c) IP address (d) HTML

20. Find the odd one out.
(a)  (b) 
(c)  (d)

21. Which of the following is a web address of a particular web page?
(a) URL (b) WWW
(c) Website (d) RUL

22. Given below is an example of a, http://www.google.com .... and "google" is the ....
(a) WiFi, browser
(b) Cyphertext, website
(c) Uniform Resource Locator, Domain name
(d) Broadband, browser

23. Who invented the term 'hypertext'?
(a) Bill Gates
(b) Steve Jobs
(c) Mark Zuckerberg
(d) Ted Nelson

24. Which of the following is a web-based tool which enables users to locate information on the World Wide Web?

(a) Search bar (b) Search engine
(c) Google search (d) Windows

25. Who invented the most popular search engine called 'Google'?

(a) Sergey Brin and Larry Page
(b) Mark Zuckerberg and Larry Page
(c) Elon Musk and Steve Jobs
(d) Steve Jobs and Mark Zuckerberg

26. To begin your search, type .... into your browser's .... and press Enter.

(a) www.google.com, Search bar
(b) www.xyz.com, Search bar
(c) www.abc.com, Address bar
(d) www.google.com, Address bar

27. Ayesha wants to search some information about Children's Day. Where should she enter the keyword of her search?

(a) Address Bar (b) Search bar
(c) Gmail (d) Menu bar

28. E-mail is a short-form for

(a) Edu mail (b) Electronic mail
(c) Electric mail (d) Ethernet mail

29. The people to which an email is sent are known as

(a) receivers (b) senders
(c) recipients (d) officers

30. In the given image, what does the term 'Cc'mean?

From: oeapi.com@gmail.com (imap.gmail.com)
To:
Cc:

(a) Carbon copy (b) Cached copy
(c) Color copy (d) Coded copy

31. Which of the following is an option to hide a certain recipient name from all other recipients?

(a) Covered Carbon Copy
(b) Concealed Carbon Copy
(c) Blind Carbon Copy
(d) Hidden Carbon Copy

32. Identify the device using given information.

It is a small box shaped device which may or may not be connected to a telephone line. It performs modulation and demodulation.
This device can be internal or external and helps the computer to send and receive data. It is provided by the ISP.

(a) Router (b) Modem
(c) Broadband (d) Dial-up

MCQs 2 Mark Questions

33. Which of the following statements about the given picture are correct?

I. It is an electronic mail service provided by Google and gives a storage capacity of around 15 gigabytes to users.It also provides a good conversation interface.

II. It is an E-commerce website known for providing various products and services. It is developed by Flipkart.

Codes

(a) Only I
(b) Only II
(c) Both the I and II
(d) Neither I nor II

34. Identify the feature using given image and description.

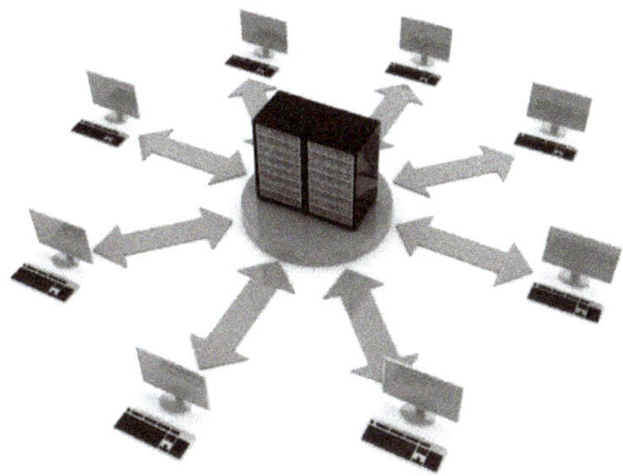

An organisation has installed the above network to connect all computers within the organisation and to protect them from external use.

The ARPANET developed by Defense Advanced Research Projects Agency is an example of it.

(a) Supernet (b) WiFi
(c) Intranet (d) Extranet

35. Match the following lists.

	List I		List II
A.	WWW	1.	Personal area network connected through infrared, bluetooth connections etc
B.	Wireless PAN	2.	Tim Berners Lee
C.	BSNL	3.	Indian ISP
D.	Facebook	4.	Social Networking Site

Codes

	A	B	C	D		A	B	C	D
(a)	2	4	1	3	(b)	2	1	4	3
(c)	2	1	3	4	(d)	1	3	2	4

Darken your choice with HB Pencil

1. ⓐ ⓑ ⓒ ⓓ	7. ⓐ ⓑ ⓒ ⓓ	13. ⓐ ⓑ ⓒ ⓓ	19. ⓐ ⓑ ⓒ ⓓ	25. ⓐ ⓑ ⓒ ⓓ	31. ⓐ ⓑ ⓒ ⓓ
2. ⓐ ⓑ ⓒ ⓓ	8. ⓐ ⓑ ⓒ ⓓ	14. ⓐ ⓑ ⓒ ⓓ	20. ⓐ ⓑ ⓒ ⓓ	26. ⓐ ⓑ ⓒ ⓓ	32. ⓐ ⓑ ⓒ ⓓ
3. ⓐ ⓑ ⓒ ⓓ	9. ⓐ ⓑ ⓒ ⓓ	15. ⓐ ⓑ ⓒ ⓓ	21. ⓐ ⓑ ⓒ ⓓ	27. ⓐ ⓑ ⓒ ⓓ	33. ⓐ ⓑ ⓒ ⓓ
4. ⓐ ⓑ ⓒ ⓓ	10. ⓐ ⓑ ⓒ ⓓ	16. ⓐ ⓑ ⓒ ⓓ	22. ⓐ ⓑ ⓒ ⓓ	28. ⓐ ⓑ ⓒ ⓓ	34. ⓐ ⓑ ⓒ ⓓ
5. ⓐ ⓑ ⓒ ⓓ	11. ⓐ ⓑ ⓒ ⓓ	17. ⓐ ⓑ ⓒ ⓓ	23. ⓐ ⓑ ⓒ ⓓ	29. ⓐ ⓑ ⓒ ⓓ	35. ⓐ ⓑ ⓒ ⓓ
6. ⓐ ⓑ ⓒ ⓓ	12. ⓐ ⓑ ⓒ ⓓ	18. ⓐ ⓑ ⓒ ⓓ	24. ⓐ ⓑ ⓒ ⓓ	30. ⓐ ⓑ ⓒ ⓓ	

Chapter 10

Latest Developments in the Field of IT

MCQs 1 Mark Questions

1. Name the operating system developed by Google for smartphones.
(a) iOS (b) Windows
(c) Android (d) Linux

2. iPhone is a line of smartphones developed by .... and they work on .... operating system.
(a) Apple Inc., iOS
(b) Microsoft, Mac
(c) IBM, Windows
(d) Google, Mac

3. Which of the following is a type of computer that can be worn on body and can monitor heartbeat, track fitness or notify about calls etc?
(a) Wrist watch (b) Mobile phone
(c) Smart ring (d) Smart watch

4. What is the full form of CCTV?
(a) Close Circuit Telecommunication
(b) Close Case Television
(c) Closed Circuit Television
(d) Close Case Telecom

5. Which type of computers are hand-held machines which work on touch-screen technology and are similar to tablets?
(a) Desktop (b) Convertible Laptop
(c) Smartphone (d) Supercomputer

6. .... is a security identification and authority device.
(a) Sensor (b) CCTV
(c) Fingerprint (d) Biometric

7. Identify the given technology which works on comparing selected facial features from the image database.

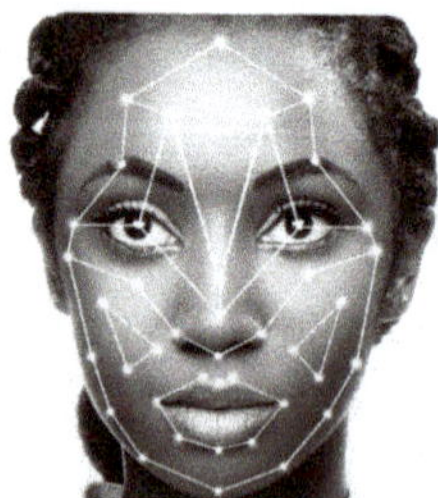

(a) DNA Recognition
(b) Iris Recognition
(c) Facial Recognition
(d) Brain Recognition

8. Touch based sensor is a type of .... recognition technique.
   (a) operating system
   (b) gesture
   (c) eye
   (d) heart

9. Which of the following is a video-sharing website which allows us to like, share and subscribe to our favourite channels?
   (a) Facebook
   (b) Instagram
   (c) Google
   (d) YouTube

10. .... is the official app store to browse and download apps for Apple devices.
   (a) Google Play Store
   (b) Apple shop
   (c) Apple Store
   (d) iStore

11. Which of the following services provide street maps, real-time traffic conditions and satellite images of locations?
   (a) Google Pay
   (b) Booking.com
   (c) Gmail
   (d) Google Maps

12. .... is a mobile application that provides GIFs and videos on small scale and lets you make collections called 'Pinboards'.
   (a) Art and craft (b) DIY
   (c) Pinterest (d) Creative interests

13. Which of the following is a popular online chat application which also allows you to make voice calls, video calls and share pictures, documents etc.?
   (a) Amazon (b) Google
   (c) WhatsApp (d) WiFi

14. Which of the following is an Indian online payment app founded by Vijay Shekhar Sharma?
   (a) Google Pay (b) Paytm
   (c) Bookmyshow (d) Paisa app

15. Raj forgot his wallet at home. He wants to pay the shopkeeper using digital payment. How can he do so?
   (a) PhonePe (b) UPI
   (c) Net Banking (d) All of these

16. Identify the first-of-its-kind domestic card payment network of India launched by the National Payments Corporation of India.
   (a) 

   (b) 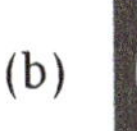 

   (c) 

   (d) 

17. .... is an online storage platform developed by Google which can be accessed anytime, anywhere with any device.
   (a) One cloud (b) Google Drive
   (c) Viber (d) Azure

18. If Swati has selected the second option from the given image then, what can she do with the document?

   Can edit
   Can comment
   Can view

   (a) Swati can edit the entire document.
   (b) Swati can only comment in the document.
   (c) Swati can only view the document and cannot make changes.
   (d) All of the above

19. 

This icon is used to create a .... in Google Drive.

(a) Shareable link (b) Document
(c) Presentation (d) Report

MCQs 2 Mark Questions

20. Identify the feature with the help of given information.

- It is a small, free standing structure which gives information or provides some service.
- It can be digital or non-digital. You may find it at airports, shopping malls, banks etc.

(a) WiFi (b) Computer
(c) Kiosk (d) ATM

21. Which of the following statements is correct about Iris Recognition System?

I. In this system, the device scans the retina of the subject and then matches it with the database. It was developed because the iris imprints almost never change in a lifetime.

II. It is one of the most secure authentication service and is used in Aadhar identification by the Government of India.

Codes

(a) Only I
(b) Only II
(c) Both I and II
(d) Neither I nor II

22. Identify the given picture with the help of the following statements.

I. It is a home video game console developed by Microsoft.

II. It comes with many accessories like wired/wireless controllers, headset, hard drives etc.

III. It has a Live feature which allows users to play, download games online. It comes in three variants: Premium, Arcade and Elite.

(a) Playstation (b) Xbox
(c) iBox (d) Nintendo

23. Which of the following statements is incorrect about the following service?

I. This service is known as MS Office365 Suite.

II. It provides web-based versions of all MS Office applications such as Word, Excel, Outlook etc.

III. It provides online chat and image sharing facility. It is developed by Tata Institute of Science.

Codes

(a) I and III (b) I and II
(c) Only II (d) All of these

24. Match the following lists.

List I (Name)	**List II** (Service)
A. 	1. App store for Android users
B. 	2. Cloud computing service by Microsoft
C. Azure	3. Tablet computer by Apple Inc.
D. iPad	4. Swipe gesture

Codes

	A	B	C	D
(a)	4	1	2	3
(b)	4	2	1	3
(c)	3	4	1	2
(d)	1	2	3	4

25. Match the following lists.

List I (Name)	**List II** (Service)
A. 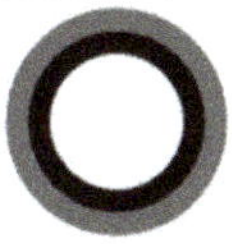	1. Online storage application
B.	2. Botnet
C. 	3. Intelligent personal assistant app
D. 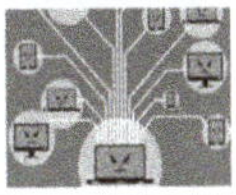	4. Instant Messenger

Codes

	A	B	C	D		A	B	C	D
(a)	2	1	4	3	(b)	1	2	4	3
(c)	3	1	4	2	(d)	1	3	2	4

Darken your choice with HB Pencil

1.	ⓐ ⓑ ⓒ ⓓ	6.	ⓐ ⓑ ⓒ ⓓ	11.	ⓐ ⓑ ⓒ ⓓ	16.	ⓐ ⓑ ⓒ ⓓ	21.	ⓐ ⓑ ⓒ ⓓ
2.	ⓐ ⓑ ⓒ ⓓ	7.	ⓐ ⓑ ⓒ ⓓ	12.	ⓐ ⓑ ⓒ ⓓ	17.	ⓐ ⓑ ⓒ ⓓ	22.	ⓐ ⓑ ⓒ ⓓ
3.	ⓐ ⓑ ⓒ ⓓ	8.	ⓐ ⓑ ⓒ ⓓ	13.	ⓐ ⓑ ⓒ ⓓ	18.	ⓐ ⓑ ⓒ ⓓ	23.	ⓐ ⓑ ⓒ ⓓ
4.	ⓐ ⓑ ⓒ ⓓ	9.	ⓐ ⓑ ⓒ ⓓ	14.	ⓐ ⓑ ⓒ ⓓ	19.	ⓐ ⓑ ⓒ ⓓ	24.	ⓐ ⓑ ⓒ ⓓ
5.	ⓐ ⓑ ⓒ ⓓ	10.	ⓐ ⓑ ⓒ ⓓ	15.	ⓐ ⓑ ⓒ ⓓ	20.	ⓐ ⓑ ⓒ ⓓ	25.	ⓐ ⓑ ⓒ ⓓ

Practice Set 1

Time : 60 Mins. Max. Marks : 60

General Instructions

1. This question paper contains 50 questions.
2. All questions are compulsory. There is no negative marking.
3. This question paper is divided into two parts; In Part I, there are 40 MCQs of 1 mark each while in Part II, there are 10 MCQs of 2 marks each.
4. Use HB pencil / Blue ball point pen to mark your choice of answer by darkening the circles on the OMR Sheet.

Part I

1. A computer is a/an
(a) mechanical device
(b) electronic device
(c) magnetic device
(d) electrical device

2. Who is the father of computer?
(a) Albert Einstein
(b) Newton
(c) Charles Babbage
(d) John Neumann

3. How do we communicate to a computer?
(a) Through verbal communication
(b) Assembly language
(c) Machine language
(d) English language

4. .... created the first digital computer in 1642.
(a) Edison (b) Blaise Pascal
(c) Ana Edward (d) John Napier

5. .... is the largest unit of information stored by a computer.
(a) Byte (b) Bit
(c) Nibble (d) Kilogram

6. Integrated circuits were used in which generation of computers?
(a) First (b) Second
(c) Third (d) Fourth

7. The fourth generation computers used which of the following?
(a) IC (b) Microprocessor
(c) Vacuum tubes (d) Transistors

8. Which of the following were introduced in fourth generation?
(a) Mainframes
(b) Supercomputers
(c) Personal computers
(d) Laptops

9. Which type of storage did third generation computers used?
(a) RAM
(b) Magnetic tape
(c) Magnetic drum
(d) Floppy disc

10. Which of the following is IBM's first generation computer?
(a) IBM 1400 (b) IBM 701
(c) IBM 1401 (d) IBM 800

11. All hardware devices are connected together by a main circuit boards known as
(a) software (b) application
(c) hard drive (d) motherboard

12. .... software consists of programs that run in the background.
(a) Hardware (b) Application
(c) System (d) Operation

13. MS Office, Photoshop, animagic are examples of
    (a) system software
    (b) operation software
    (c) utility software
    (d) application software

14. Which of the following devices accepts text, images etc. from computer and then displays them on paper?
    (a) Scanner (b) Printer
    (c) Speaker (d) Monitor

15. What is the default file format of Windows Media Player?
    (a) .wap (b) .wmp
    (c) .wma (d) .mp3

16. Which option would you click to change windows theme?
    (a) Cortana
    (b) Control panel
    (c) Device driver
    (d) Personalisation

17. The .... helps you to end tasks if your computer is not responding.
    (a) manager
    (b) program counter
    (c) system software
    (d) task manager

18. In Windows 10, what is the shortcut to open programs pinned to taskbar?
    (a) Alt +123 (b) Ctrl+123
    (c) Windows+123 (d) Shift +123

19. In MS Word, which menu has word count option?
    (a) Edit menu (b) Tools menu
    (c) Insert menu (d) View menu

20. What is the shortcut key to check spelling in MS Word?
    (a) F5 (b) F9
    (c) F12 (d) F7

21. Which of the following is not available in print dialog box of MS Word?
    (a) Print preview
    (b) Print selected text
    (c) Collate copies
    (d) Print a file more than once

22. What displays a spelling mistake in a document?
    (a) Green line (b) Red line
    (c) Blue line (d) None of these

23. What is the purpose of drawing tool box in MS Word?
    (a) To place clip art
    (b) To draw shapes
    (c) To draw tables
    (d) To write text

24. What is the basic file of MS Excel?
    (a) Presentation (b) Workbook
    (c) Word (d) All of these

25. Which of the following is the last column of an excel worksheet?
    (a) XFD (b) AV
    (c) DV (d) XV

26. What combination keys will help you select the entire row of the active cell?
    (a) Ctrl + F1
    (b) Alt + Spacebar
    (c) Ctrl + Spacebar
    (d) Shift + Spacebar

27. Which shortcut key will access the entire column of an active cell?
    (a) Ctrl + Spacebar (b) Alt + Spacebar
    (c) Ctrl + F1 (d) Alt + F1

28. Which wizard of MS PowerPoint contains a series of questions for designing a presentation?
    (a) Blank presentation
    (b) Design templates
    (c) Auto fill
    (d) Auto content

29. What enables you to change the background of a slide?
(a) Insert Background
(b) Format Background
(c) View Background
(d) Tools Background

30. How many screens does the Auto Content wizard contain?
(a) 3-5 (b) 8-12
(c) 6-8 (d) 7-8

31. .... is a high level programming language.
(a) C Programming
(b) MS Word
(c) Q Basic
(d) Both (a) and (c)

32. The data values in Q Basic program that cannot be changed or altered during the programs execution.
(a) Character Set (b) Variable
(c) String (d) Constants

33. Which of the following operators will combine two string constants?
(a) - (b) +
(c) * (d) ++

34. Character set in QBASIC includes
(a) numeric digits
(b) letters
(c) special characters
(d) All of the above

35. Which of the following is not an internet connection service?
(a) ISDN (b) DSL
(c) UPS (d) Wi-Fi

36. This word art contribute is commonly seen during verification. This is known as
(a) Crypt (b) Auto Text
(c) Code (d) Captcha

37. Web addresses can be written as words or as numbers. For example: www.sofworld.org might have an address number of 63.141.53.0. What are these numbers called?
(a) Uniform Resource Locator Number
(b) Internet Protocol Address
(c) File Transfer Protocol Address
(d) ISP Number

38. Which app can be used to setup, connect multiple devices in your home?
(a) Google Earth (b) Facebook
(c) Amazon (d) Google Home

39. Which of the following is recognised as global positioning system?

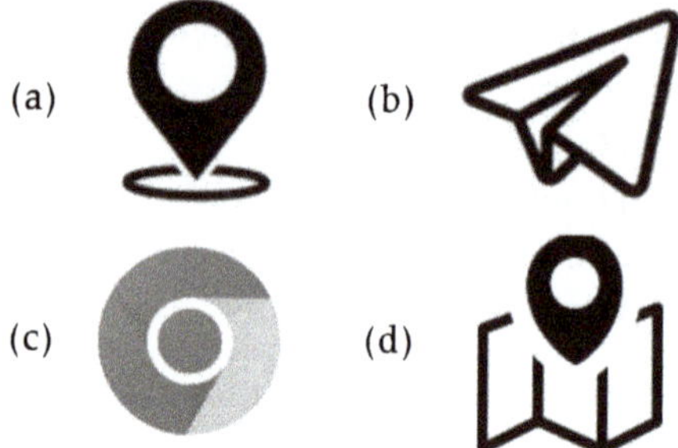

40. Which of the following social media apps has a feature known as 'Reels' where users can share short videos?
(a) Facebook (b) Instagram
(c) Twitter (d) Tik-tok

MCQs 2 Marks Questions

41. When talking about networking and Internet, what is a port?
I. An external output device.
II. An input device.
III. It's the protocol that e-mail messages have to follow to travel over the Internet.
IV. It's a data connection that allows information transfer to and from a specific server process.

Codes

(a) I and II (b) I and IV
(c) II and III (d) Only IV

42. Match the following lists.

	List I		List II
A.	MS Word	1.	Customised
B.	Airline reservation	2.	General purpose
C.	Antivirus	3.	System software
D.	Device driver	4.	Utility

Codes

	A	B	C	D		A	B	C	D
(a)	1	2	3	4	(b)	4	3	1	2
(c)	3	4	2	1	(d)	2	1	4	3

43. You can add new toolbars to your taskbar by

I. right clicking taskbar then clicking toolbar

II. going to control panel then clicking toolbar

III. right click taskbar then choose task manager-toolbar

Codes

(a) Only I (b) II and III
(c) I and III (d) None of these

44. What does the cell with the arrow mark represent?

(a) Sheet tab (b) Cell pointer
(c) Active sheet (d) Workbook

45. What should be done to make one section of slides in a presentation use a different design template from that of the other slides?

(a) Select the slide thumbnails in that section and select the duplicate slide.

(b) Select the slide thumbnails in that section and apply a different design template.

(c) Select one of the slides in the section you want to change, customise the fonts and colors and use the Format Painter to apply those styles to the other slides in the section.

(d) Both (a) and (b)

46. What does the given dialog box represent?

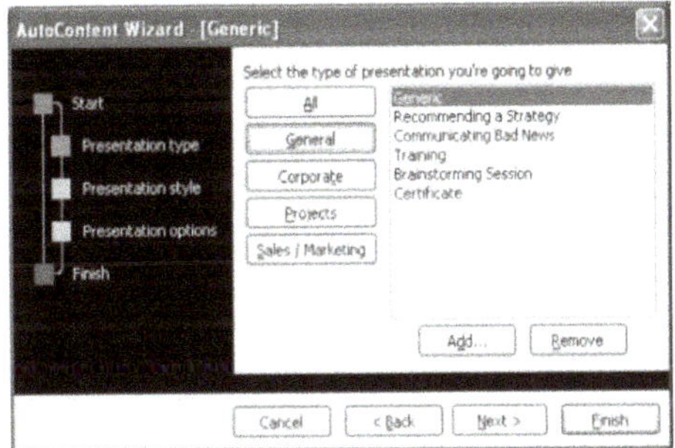

(a) Blank presentation

(b) Auto Content wizard

(c) Design template

(d) A slide in outline view

47. Which of the following statements is not true for a variable?

(a) Variable name can begin with a letter of the English alphabet.

(b) Variable name can begin with a special character.

(c) Variable name cannot be a reserved word.

(d) Name of variables that store alphanumeric value must end with a $ sign.

48. Match the following lists.

List I	List II
A. ISP	1. Ask .com
B. Search Engine	2. AIRCEL
C. Web browser	3. e

Codes

	A	B	C		A	B	C
(a)	2	1	3	(b)	1	3	2
(c)	2	3	1	(d)	3	2	1

49. Which of the following is a cloud computing platform provided by Microsoft ?

I. Delta II. Drive
III. Azure IV. Alexa

Codes

(a) I and II (b) Only II
(c) Only III (d) II and III

50. Which of the following is an AI based app designed to evaluate and give feedback on your English pronunciation and fluency?

I. Alexa
II. ELSA speak
III. Siri
IV. Google assistant

Codes

(a) Only I (b) Only II
(c) I and II (d) I and III

Darken your choice with HB Pencil

1.	ⓐ ⓑ ⓒ ⓓ	10.	ⓐ ⓑ ⓒ ⓓ	19.	ⓐ ⓑ ⓒ ⓓ	28.	ⓐ ⓑ ⓒ ⓓ	37.	ⓐ ⓑ ⓒ ⓓ	46.	ⓐ ⓑ ⓒ ⓓ
2.	ⓐ ⓑ ⓒ ⓓ	11.	ⓐ ⓑ ⓒ ⓓ	20.	ⓐ ⓑ ⓒ ⓓ	29.	ⓐ ⓑ ⓒ ⓓ	38.	ⓐ ⓑ ⓒ ⓓ	47.	ⓐ ⓑ ⓒ ⓓ
3.	ⓐ ⓑ ⓒ ⓓ	12.	ⓐ ⓑ ⓒ ⓓ	21.	ⓐ ⓑ ⓒ ⓓ	30.	ⓐ ⓑ ⓒ ⓓ	39.	ⓐ ⓑ ⓒ ⓓ	48.	ⓐ ⓑ ⓒ ⓓ
4.	ⓐ ⓑ ⓒ ⓓ	13.	ⓐ ⓑ ⓒ ⓓ	22.	ⓐ ⓑ ⓒ ⓓ	31.	ⓐ ⓑ ⓒ ⓓ	40.	ⓐ ⓑ ⓒ ⓓ	49.	ⓐ ⓑ ⓒ ⓓ
5.	ⓐ ⓑ ⓒ ⓓ	14.	ⓐ ⓑ ⓒ ⓓ	23.	ⓐ ⓑ ⓒ ⓓ	32.	ⓐ ⓑ ⓒ ⓓ	41.	ⓐ ⓑ ⓒ ⓓ	50.	ⓐ ⓑ ⓒ ⓓ
6.	ⓐ ⓑ ⓒ ⓓ	15.	ⓐ ⓑ ⓒ ⓓ	24.	ⓐ ⓑ ⓒ ⓓ	33.	ⓐ ⓑ ⓒ ⓓ	42.	ⓐ ⓑ ⓒ ⓓ		
7.	ⓐ ⓑ ⓒ ⓓ	16.	ⓐ ⓑ ⓒ ⓓ	25.	ⓐ ⓑ ⓒ ⓓ	34.	ⓐ ⓑ ⓒ ⓓ	43.	ⓐ ⓑ ⓒ ⓓ		
8.	ⓐ ⓑ ⓒ ⓓ	17.	ⓐ ⓑ ⓒ ⓓ	26.	ⓐ ⓑ ⓒ ⓓ	35.	ⓐ ⓑ ⓒ ⓓ	44.	ⓐ ⓑ ⓒ ⓓ		
9.	ⓐ ⓑ ⓒ ⓓ	18.	ⓐ ⓑ ⓒ ⓓ	27.	ⓐ ⓑ ⓒ ⓓ	36.	ⓐ ⓑ ⓒ ⓓ	45.	ⓐ ⓑ ⓒ ⓓ		

Practice Set 2

Time : 60 Mins. Max. Marks : 60

General Instructions

1. This question paper contains 50 questions.
2. All questions are compulsory. There is no negative marking.
3. This question paper is divided into two parts; In Part I, there are 40 MCQs of 1 mark each while in Part II, there are 10 MCQs of 2 marks each.
4. Use HB pencil / Blue ball point pen to mark your choice of answer by darkening the circles on the OMR Sheet.

Part I

1. UNIVAC is an example of .... generation computer.
   (a) first (b) second
   (c) third (d) fourth

2. Which of the following statements is/are true about fourth generation computer?
   (a) Fourth generation computers used microprocessor.
   (b) Microprocessor generally consists of thousands of integrated circuit.
   (c) These computers used assembly language.
   (d) Both (a) and (b)

3. You can take computer output in two mode hardcopy and softcopy. Which of the following output devices provides hardcopy?
   (a) Dot matrix printer
   (b) Daisy wheel printer
   (c) Ink jet printer
   (d) All of the above

4. Which bar contain name of the current program at its left side and control button at it right?
   (a) Menu bar (b) Status bar
   (c) Title bar (d) Taskbar

5. What is the mean of the Booting in the system?
   (a) Restarting computer
   (b) Install the program
   (c) To scan
   (d) To turn off

6. The central processing unit is located in the
   (a) Hard disk (b) System unit
   (c) Memory unit (d) Monitor

7. What is five main components of a computer system?
   (a) CPU, CD-ROM, Mouse, Keyboard, Sound card
   (b) Memory, Video card, Monitor, Software, Hardware
   (c) Modem, Keyboard, Word Processor, Printer, Screen
   (d) CPU, Memory, System bus, Input, Output

8. What is the use of the computer port?
   (a) Download the file via the internet
   (b) To connect with other devices
   (c) To reduce the internet speed
   (d) None of the above

9. Batch processing and multiprogramming operating systems were used in these computers.
   (a) Second generation (b) Third generation
   (c) Fourth generation (d) Both (a) and (b)

10. The fifth generation uses .... programming languages.
(a) C, C++, Java, .Net, etc.
(b) OPS5 and Mercury etc
(c) COBOL
(d) FORTRAN, BASIC

11. A business card reader uses .... technology to convert text on business card to typed text on the computer.
(a) Impact
(b) MICR
(c) Optical Character Recognition
(d) Optical Mark Reader

12. Windows system implements the
(a) Graphical User Interface
(b) User Interface
(c) Resource Interface
(d) Computer Interface

13. Which desktop feature has been included in windows 10 that was omitted from windows 8?
(a) Gadgets (b) Start menu
(c) Recycle bin (d) Task view

14. Which of the key is used to close the active window?
(a) Ctrl+F4 (b) Ctrl+F5
(c) Alt+F6 (d) None of these

15. The shortcut key to open a task manager is
(a) Alt + F1 (b) Ctrl + Shift + ESC
(c) Alt + Tab (d) F1

16. The windows feature is the ability of computer to automatically configure a new hardware component is that
(a) auto detect
(b) plug and play
(c) add remove hardware
(d) None of the above

17. What are the steps to format a page in MS Word?
(a) Page layout Tab → page setup
(b) View → page setup
(c) Format → page setup
(d) Insert → page setup

18. While working with MS Word, which command is used to find the number of paragraphs in the currently opened document?
(a) Tools → Track changes
(b) Tools → Compare and merge document
(c) Review Tab → Word count
(d) Tools → Auto summarised

19. Which tool in MS Word shows margins and tab settings for the selected text?
(a) Align text (b) Format painter
(c) Ruler (d) Paragraph

20. While working in MS-Word, what is the use of Shift + F7 keys?
(a) To popup Spelling and Grammar check window.
(b) To popup Format dialog box.
(c) To popup Thesaurus dialog box.
(d) To popup Find and Replace dialog box.

21. What is the component of MS-Excel window given called?

(a) Standard tool bar (b) Formula bar
(c) Title bar (d) Chart bar

22. Which steps would you follow to start MS Excel?
(a) Start → All Programs → MS Excel
(b) Start → All Programs → Microsoft office → MS Excel
(c) Click on MS Excel icon of MS Office shortcut tool bar
(d) All of the above

23. Which of these is/are the data types of MS Excel?
(a) Numbers (b) Text
(c) Formulae (d) Both (a) and (b)

24. Which shortcut key will access the entire column of an active cell?
(a) Ctrl + Spacebar (b) Alt + Spacebar
(c) Ctrl + F1 (d) Alt + F1

25. Which key should be pressed to activate extend indicator (EXT) in status bar?
(a) F5 (b) F7 (c) F8 (d) F11

26. Which of the following views displays miniature representation of slides of a presentation?
(a) Slide show (b) Slide sorter view
(c) Outline view (d) Slide view

27. In PowerPoint, what action will take place when you double click on the title bar?
(a) PowerPoint application will be closed.
(b) Active presentation of PowerPoint will be closed.
(c) The presentation becomes error free.
(d) The presentation is minimized.

28. Which of the following provides readymade background designs to your presentations in PowerPoint?
(a) Blank presentation
(b) Slide show
(c) Auto Content wizard
(d) Design templates

29. Which of the following statement is correct?
(a) Ping Pong is an example of computer virus.
(b) Virus is a easily detectable hardware.
(c) Without any human action, Trojan horse can replicate itself.
(d) All of the above

30. Web addresses can be written as words or as numbers. For example: www.sofworld.org might have an address number of 63.141.53.0. What are these numbers called?
(a) Uniform Resource Locator Number
(b) Internet Protocol Address
(c) File Transfer Protocol Address
(d) ISP Number

31. .... is a web browser developed by Apple Inc.

32. Identify valid email address.
(a) t4tutorials@.com
(b) t4tutorials.com
(c) t4@t4tutorials.com
(d) t4tutorials@books

33. Which of the following is like a raw copy of your email message which can be edited anytime?
(a) Draft
(b) Outbox
(c) Spam
(d) trash

34. What is included in an E-mail address?
(a) Domain name followed by user's name.
(b) User name followed by domain name.
(c) User name followed by postal address.
(d) User name followed by street address.

35. You can press.......... to select the File Menu. Then from the pull-down Menu, Select New option by pressing............. .

36. "My name is Anuraag" is an invalid string constant because
(a) It is not enclosed within quotation marks.
(b) Quotation marks are not allowed inside the string data.
(c) Closing quotation mark is missing at the end.
(d) None of the above

37. Which of the following is a platform where you can share your opinions and content online as well as offline?
(a) Windows (b) Chrome
(c) Blog (d) Amazon

38. Find the odd one out.
(a) Facebook (b) WhatsApp
(c) Reddit (d) Botnet

39. .... is a periodic email sent by an organisation or a person sharing latest developments and news about them.
(a) Blog (b) Newsletter
(c) Update (d) Postcard

40. Which of the following is a network of computers infected by malware that are under the control of a single attacking party?
(a) Malware (b) Botnet
(c) Virus (d) Antivirus

Part II

41. What would be the output of the following code?

```
CLS
LET NAME = 5
PRINT "I am"; NAME; "AND"
```

(a) Iam 5 ANU
(b) I am 5 AND
(c) I am5ANU
(d) Iam5ANU

42. Which of the following statements is true?
I. Super computers are the fastest computers.
II. Charles Babbage invented Analytical Engine.

Codes
(a) Only I (b) Only II
(c) Both I and II (d) Neither I nor II

43. Which of the following statements hold(s) true regarding processor?
I. It is a microchip implanted in a system unit that processes instructions sent to it by the computer.
II. It is manufactured by corporations such as Intel.

Codes
(a) Only I (b) Only II
(c) Both I and II (d) Neither I nor II

44. Identify the terms 'X' and 'Y' with the help of given information in the given diagram.
X. It is a type of software that directly interacts with the hardware.
Y. It is a type of software that directly Interacts with user.

(a) Programming System, Operating System
(b) Interpreter, Operating System
(c) Application, Operating System
(d) Operating System, Application software

45. Which of the following statements is not true about System Software?
(a) It is designed to operate the computer hardware.
(b) It provides basic functionality to the computer.
(c) They are simple programs designed to accomplish certain tasks.
(d) It is responsible for managing a variety of independent hardware components.

46. Identify the following type of printer with the help of given information.

X. They use typewriting printing mechanism, wherein a hammer strikes the paper through a ribbon in order to produce output.

Y. They do not touch paper while printing. They use chemical, heat or electric signal to etch the symbols on paper.

Codes

(a) X - Impact printer, Y - Non-impact printer

(b) X - Common printer, Y - Uncommon printer

(c) X - Non-impact printer, Y - Impact printer

(d) X - Uncommon printer, Y - Common printer

47. Identify the sequence of steps used to add a picture from file into a PowerPoint presentation.

(a) Choose the menu option Insert → Picture → Clip Art

(b) Choose the menu option Insert → Picture → From file

(c) Choose the menu option Insert → Add Picture → From file

(d) Choose the menu option Insert → Add Picture → Auto shapes

48. What would be the output of the given code?

```
CLS
LET b = 4
IF b MOD 2 = 0 THEN
PRINT "Even Number"
ELSE
PRINT "ODD Number"
END IF
```

(a) Even Number

(b) ODD Number

(c) ODD Number
Even Number

(d) Even Number
ODD Number

49. Which of the following is an correct example of LET statement?

(a) LET B = 274

(b) LET RATE = 25.25

(c) LET A $ = "BASIC"

(d) All of the above

50. Which of the following is true about RAzorpay?

I. It provides access to all types of modes of payments.

II. It was founded in 2015.

Codes

(a) Only I (b) Only II

(c) Both I and II (d) Neither I nor II

Darken your choice with HB Pencil

1. ⓐ ⓑ ⓒ ⓓ	10. ⓐ ⓑ ⓒ ⓓ	19. ⓐ ⓑ ⓒ ⓓ	28. ⓐ ⓑ ⓒ ⓓ	37. ⓐ ⓑ ⓒ ⓓ	46. ⓐ ⓑ ⓒ ⓓ
2. ⓐ ⓑ ⓒ ⓓ	11. ⓐ ⓑ ⓒ ⓓ	20. ⓐ ⓑ ⓒ ⓓ	29. ⓐ ⓑ ⓒ ⓓ	38. ⓐ ⓑ ⓒ ⓓ	47. ⓐ ⓑ ⓒ ⓓ
3. ⓐ ⓑ ⓒ ⓓ	12. ⓐ ⓑ ⓒ ⓓ	21. ⓐ ⓑ ⓒ ⓓ	30. ⓐ ⓑ ⓒ ⓓ	39. ⓐ ⓑ ⓒ ⓓ	48. ⓐ ⓑ ⓒ ⓓ
4. ⓐ ⓑ ⓒ ⓓ	13. ⓐ ⓑ ⓒ ⓓ	22. ⓐ ⓑ ⓒ ⓓ	31. ⓐ ⓑ ⓒ ⓓ	40. ⓐ ⓑ ⓒ ⓓ	49. ⓐ ⓑ ⓒ ⓓ
5. ⓐ ⓑ ⓒ ⓓ	14. ⓐ ⓑ ⓒ ⓓ	23. ⓐ ⓑ ⓒ ⓓ	32. ⓐ ⓑ ⓒ ⓓ	41. ⓐ ⓑ ⓒ ⓓ	50. ⓐ ⓑ ⓒ ⓓ
6. ⓐ ⓑ ⓒ ⓓ	15. ⓐ ⓑ ⓒ ⓓ	24. ⓐ ⓑ ⓒ ⓓ	33. ⓐ ⓑ ⓒ ⓓ	42. ⓐ ⓑ ⓒ ⓓ	
7. ⓐ ⓑ ⓒ ⓓ	16. ⓐ ⓑ ⓒ ⓓ	25. ⓐ ⓑ ⓒ ⓓ	34. ⓐ ⓑ ⓒ ⓓ	43. ⓐ ⓑ ⓒ ⓓ	
8. ⓐ ⓑ ⓒ ⓓ	17. ⓐ ⓑ ⓒ ⓓ	26. ⓐ ⓑ ⓒ ⓓ	35. ⓐ ⓑ ⓒ ⓓ	44. ⓐ ⓑ ⓒ ⓓ	
9. ⓐ ⓑ ⓒ ⓓ	18. ⓐ ⓑ ⓒ ⓓ	27. ⓐ ⓑ ⓒ ⓓ	36. ⓐ ⓑ ⓒ ⓓ	45. ⓐ ⓑ ⓒ ⓓ	

Practice Set 3

Time : 60 Mins. Max. Marks : 60

General Instructions

1. This question paper contains 50 questions.
2. All questions are compulsory. There is no negative marking.
3. This question paper is divided into two parts; In Part I, there are 40 MCQs of 1 mark each while in Part II, there are 10 MCQs of 2 marks each.
4. Use HB pencil / Blue ball point pen to mark your choice of answer by darkening the circles on the OMR Sheet.

Part I

1. Neha has typed the word 'are' instead of 'or' in the document. What should she do to change all the words that are typed incorrectly?

(a) Use arrow key to find every incorrect word and correct it.
(b) Use find and replace function to find every incorrect word and replace it.
(c) Re-type the whole document carefully.
(d) Highlight all the incorrect words.

2. What is the shortcut key to increase the font size of selected text in MS-Word?

(a) Ctrl + Shift + G (b) Ctrl + Shift+ >
(c) Ctrl + Shift + < (d) Ctrl + Shift + X

3. What happens when the combinational keys Ctrl+2 is pressed?

(a) It selects all the contents of the document.
(b) It aligns the selected text to the centre of the screen.
(c) It opens 'Save as' dialog box.
(d) Changes a line, a paragraph or all highlighted text to have double spacing.

4. What is the purpose of word wrap feature of MS-Word?

(a) To introduce a new line.
(b) To bring the text to the next line, if it goes beyond the right margin.
(c) To keep a part of a word in the current file and the remaining in the next file.
(d) To align the lines in a paragraph.

5. Which cell in the Excel window is active?

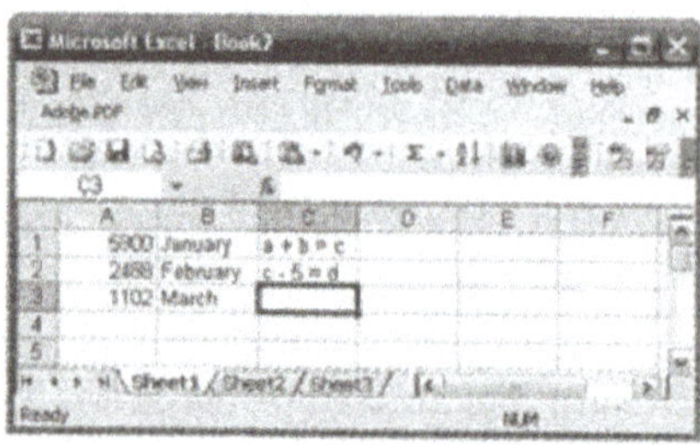

(a) C3 (b) B2 (c) A6 (d) D1

6. What is the component of MS-Excel window given called?

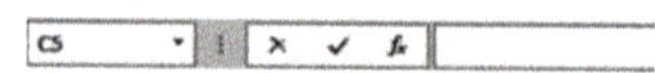

(a) Standard tool bar
(b) Formula bar
(c) Title bar
(d) Chart bar

7. Which steps would you follow to insert a work sheet in your work book?

(a) File → New
(b) Home tab → Cells group → Insert → Insert Sheet
(c) Data Insert → Worksheet
(d) All of the above

8. What are the steps to insert a new row in a worksheet?

(a) Edit → New → Row
(b) File → New → Row
(c) Format → Row
(d) Home tab → Cells group → Insert → Insert sheet rows

9. Which button does X in the given picture denote?

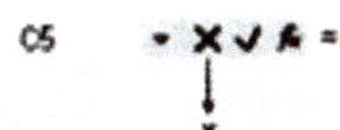

(a) Enter (b) Cancel (c) OK (d) Save

10. What are the special effects used for introducing slides in a presentation called?
(a) Effects (b) Custom animations
(c) Transitions (d) Present animations

11. Which of the following audio formats can be inserted into a PowerPoint presentation?
(a) .mp3 (b) .avi
(c) .mov (d) .wmv

12. What does 'Design' tab do in MS PowerPoint?
(a) It changes the content of the slide.
(b) It adds functionality to the slide.
(c) It changes the look of the slide without changing the content.
(d) It changes the alignment of the content in the slide.

13. In the web address http//:www.myhomepage.com/pictures/myschool/ClassVI.jpg
What does /myschool/ indicate?
(a) The name of the image on the website.
(b) It is the URL.
(c) The folder where ClassVI.jpg will be found.
(d) The homepage image for the website www.myhomepage.com.

14. The given logo is of Wikipedia. It is

(a) a free online encyclopedia
(b) a translator software
(c) a web browser software
(d) a search engine application

15. A block of text automatically added to an outgoing mail is
(a) attachment (b) signature
(c) encryption (d) decryption

16. To send a received email to another person you should
(a) delete it (b) reply to it
(c) forward it (d) copy it

17. Given below is an arithmetic expression. Which of the following parts of the expression will be calculated first in QBASIC?

A+B/5*C-D

(a) B/3 (b) DΛ2
(c) A+B (d) 5*C

18. What is the output of the given program?

```
CLS
LET X$ = "Welcome"
LET Y$ = "to"
LET Z$ = "India"
PRINT X$;Y$;Z$
```

(a) Welcome to India
(b) Welcome toIndia
(c) Welcometo India
(d) WelcometoIndia

19. Which of the following numeric variables is Invalid?
(a) A@ (b) MG
(c) PS5 (d) Both (b) and (c)

20. You can select My Computer icon and press Alt + Enter to
(a) delete it from desktop permanently.
(b) open it in Explorer mode.
(c) open System Properties dialog box.
(d) pin it on Start menu.

21. The ...... provides information about hardware installation, configuration and hardware status.
(a) device manager
(b) control panel
(c) add new hardware
(d) program manager

22. Which of the following is group of programs?
(a) Accessories (b) Paint
(c) Word (d) All of these

23. Which program runs first after booting the computer and loading the GUI?
(a) Desktop Manager (b) File Manager
(c) Windows Explorer (d) Authentication

24. In Windows 10,which of the following enables you to take a screenshot of the entire window and save ?
(a) Shift + prtscre
(b) alt+prtscr
(c) Ctrl+prtscr
(d) Windows key + prtscr

25. Ctrl, Shift and Alt are known as .... keys.
(a) function (b) modifier
(c) alphanumeric (d) adjustment

26. Which of the following is a combination of input-output devices?
(a) VDU (b) Keyboard
(c) Printer (d) Modem

27. I am having a large video - around 4 GB size which I want to copy from my laptop to my desktop. Which of the following storage medium is best suited for transferring the video to the desktop computer?
(a) 3.5 inch floppy disk
(b) 5.25 inch floppy disk
(c) 8 GB pen drive
(d) A CD ROM which has only around 10% space available

28. Which of the following components of CPU controls input/output devices, generate control signals to the other components of the computer such as read and write signals and performs the execution of instruction?
(a) ALU (b) Accumulator
(c) Control Unit (d) Both (a) and (c)

29. Select the name of the generation in which Time sharing, Real-time, Networks, Distributed Operating System was used.
(a) First (b) Fourth
(c) Fifth (d) Second

30. Select the name of the generation that used CD ROM for the first time.
(a) Second Generation
(b) Third Generation
(c) Fourth Generation
(d) Fifth Generation

31. Select the three decisions making actions performed by the ALU of a computer.
(a) Less than (b) Greater than
(c) Equal to (d) All of these

32. Computer is free from fatigue and boredom. This quality is called
(a) accuracy (b) speed
(c) versatility (d) diligence

33. Instructions and memory address are represented by .... in a computer.
(a) parity bit
(b) numeric code
(c) binary code
(d) binary alphabets

34. A hybrid computer resembles
(a) analog computer
(b) digital computer
(c) Both analog and digital computers
(d) None of the above

35. What is required when more than one person uses a central computer at the same time?
(a) Keyboard (b) Terminal
(c) CPU (d) Monitor

36. .... is a method of creating a three-dimensional object layer by layer using a computer aided design.
(a) Textile (b) Scanning
(c) 3D printing (d) 2D printing

37. It is a latest development in IT where the advertisers show their ads in a particular region.

(a) Satellite ads (b) Geomap
(c) Earthads (d) Geotargetting

38. DRIVE OS is a software used in

(a) automatic cars (b) driverless cars
(c) in-driver cars (d) two wheelers

39. Find the odd one out.

(a) 

(b) 

(c) 
(d) 

40. Which of the following is a discussion platform where you can listen to hosts and guests discuss various topics and you can also download the contents?

(a) Bookmark (b) Podcast
(c) Talkshow (d) Reality show

Part II

41. Determine the sequence of events in mail merge in MS Word.

I. Create main document
II. Perform merging
III. Relate it to data source
IV. Select the desired fields

Codes

(a) I, III, II, IV (b) I, II, IV, III
(c) IV, III, I, II (d) I, III, IV, II

42. Which of the following is not correct?

(a) PowerPoint allows the insertion pictures and cartoons into a slide.
(b) PowerPoint allows the modification of the size and location of pictures.
(c) Tables cannot be used to display data in a columnar form.
(d) Organisation charts are typically used for representing organisational hierarchy.

43. Using a custom animation effect, how will you make text in fly mode appear on a slide?

(a) Apply the animation scheme fade in one by one.
(b) Apply an entrance effect and then set it to by letter in the effect options dialog box.
(c) Apply the fly mode option in entrance effect to the text.
(d) Apply an exit effect and set it to by letter in the effect options.

44. Match the following lists.

List I	List II
A. Negatives Search	1. "I" m feeling lucky?
B. Opens the first and most	2. "–" relevant website
C. Phrase search	3. " "

Codes

	A	B	C
(a)	1	2	3
(b)	2	3	1
(c)	3	1	2
(d)	2	1	3

45. Study the given QBASIC code carefully and answer the question that follow.

```
CLS
LET B=1
ONE : IF B < 40 THEN GOTO TWO ELSE
GOTO THREE
TWO : PRINT b
B = B + 2
GOTO ONE
THREE : END
```

What will this QBASIC code print on screen?

(a) Even numbers between 1 and 40
(b) Odd numbers between 1 and 40
(c) Even numbers between 1 and 41
(d) Counting from 1 to 40

46. Which among the following is an invalid numeric constants and why?

0.75	–99.09	48/A
I	II	III

(a) Only I because decimals are not allowed
(b) Only II because negative integers are not allowed
(c) Only III because alphanumeric are not allowed
(d) None of the above

47. Complete the given diagram by replacing the X, Y and Z with the following options.

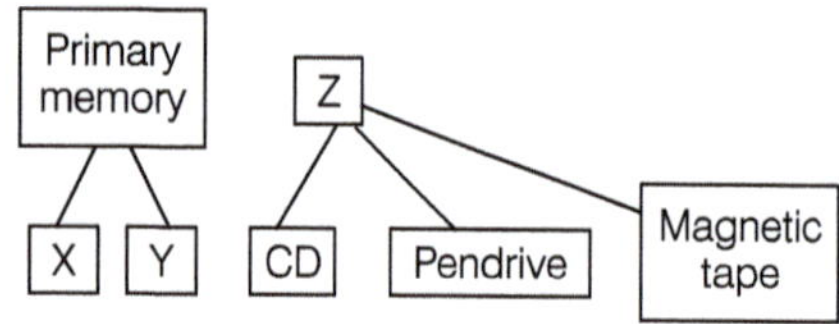

(a) X - RAM; Y - ROM; Z - Auxiliary memory
(b) X - RAM; Y - ROM; Z - Secondary memory
(c) X - Hard disk; Y - RAM; Z - Secondary memory
(d) Both (a) and (b)

48. Which of the following statements is valid?
I. Lady Augusta is the first programmer.
II. ADA is a programming language.

Codes

(a) Only I (b) Only II
(c) Both I and II (d) Neither I nor II

49. ASCII and EBCDIC are popular coding systems. The full-form of EBCDIC is
I. Extended Binary Coded Decimal Interchange Code
II. Extended Bit Coded Decimal Interchange Code
III. Extended Binary Centred Data Interchange Code
IV. Extended Byte Coded Decimal Information Code

Codes

(a) Only I (b) I and II
(c) Only IV (d) None of these

50. Identify the following.
I. It was a special purpose computer.
II. It was the first automatic electronic digital computer built in 1942.

(a) EDSAC (b) UNIVAC
(c) IBM (d) ABC

Darken your choice with HB Pencil

1.	(a) (b) (c) (d)	10.	(a) (b) (c) (d)	19.	(a) (b) (c) (d)	28.	(a) (b) (c) (d)	37.	(a) (b) (c) (d)	46.	(a) (b) (c) (d)
2.	(a) (b) (c) (d)	11.	(a) (b) (c) (d)	20.	(a) (b) (c) (d)	29.	(a) (b) (c) (d)	38.	(a) (b) (c) (d)	47.	(a) (b) (c) (d)
3.	(a) (b) (c) (d)	12.	(a) (b) (c) (d)	21.	(a) (b) (c) (d)	30.	(a) (b) (c) (d)	39.	(a) (b) (c) (d)	48.	(a) (b) (c) (d)
4.	(a) (b) (c) (d)	13.	(a) (b) (c) (d)	22.	(a) (b) (c) (d)	31.	(a) (b) (c) (d)	40.	(a) (b) (c) (d)	49.	(a) (b) (c) (d)
5.	(a) (b) (c) (d)	14.	(a) (b) (c) (d)	23.	(a) (b) (c) (d)	32.	(a) (b) (c) (d)	41.	(a) (b) (c) (d)	50.	(a) (b) (c) (d)
6.	(a) (b) (c) (d)	15.	(a) (b) (c) (d)	24.	(a) (b) (c) (d)	33.	(a) (b) (c) (d)	42.	(a) (b) (c) (d)		
7.	(a) (b) (c) (d)	16.	(a) (b) (c) (d)	25.	(a) (b) (c) (d)	34.	(a) (b) (c) (d)	43.	(a) (b) (c) (d)		
8.	(a) (b) (c) (d)	17.	(a) (b) (c) (d)	26.	(a) (b) (c) (d)	35.	(a) (b) (c) (d)	44.	(a) (b) (c) (d)		
9.	(a) (b) (c) (d)	18.	(a) (b) (c) (d)	27.	(a) (b) (c) (d)	36.	(a) (b) (c) (d)	45.	(a) (b) (c) (d)		

Answers *and* Explanations

CHAPTER 1

1. (a)	**2.** (d)	**3.** (a)	**4.** (b)	**5.** (b)
6. (b)	**7.** (b)	**8.** (d)	**9.** (c)	**10.** (b)
11. (c)	**12.** (c)	**13.** (d)	**14.** (b)	**15.** (b)
16. (a)	**17.** (c)	**18.** (b)	**19.** (c)	**20.** (a)
21. (c)	**22.** (c)	**23.** (a)	**24.** (c)	**25.** (a)
26. (c)	**27.** (c)			

28. (c) PDP-8 is a 12-bit first commercially successful minicomputer that was produced by Digital Equipment Corporation (DEC).

29. (c) A mainframe computer can process a millions of instructions per second hence, its speed is measured in MIPS.
Tablet computers are compact in size hence, they are microcomputer.

30. (b) An assembler program converts instructions into a pattern of bits so that the computer can easily process them.

31. (a) ENIAC was the first programmable, electronic, general-purpose digital computer. It was able to solve a large class of Numerical problems.
ENIAC contained thousands of vacuum tubes and several tubes burned out almost everyday, leaving ENIAC non-functional half the time.

32. (d) Trinity was the first supercomputer. PARAM Yuva II was developed by CDAC. Colossus was an electronic and digital computer that was developed by Tommy Flowers.

33. (c) Interpreter and compiler both converts high level language to low level language. But interpreter translates one statement at a time and compiler translates the entire program to low level in a single run.

CHAPTER 2

1. (c)	**2.** (b)	**3.** (d)	**4.** (a)	**5.** (a)
6. (b)	**7.** (c)	**8.** (b)	**9.** (d)	**10.** (d)
11. (d)	**12.** (d)	**13.** (d)	**14.** (a)	**15.** (b)
16. (b)				

17. (c) ENIAC was the first electronic computer which was quite fast but generated a lot of heat.

18. (d) Playstation is popular company which makes home video game consoles.

19. (d) **20.** (d)

21. (d) Mac is a fourth generation family of computers. The original Mac was the first mass-marketed personal computer.

22. (d) Herman Hollerith developed Hollerith's machine that was capable of reading numbers and characters.

23. (a) Difference engine was an automatic mechanical calculator created by Charles Babbage. Napier's bones was a manually-operated calculator created by John Napier. Analytical engine was also developed by Charles Babbage. It was mechanical calculator and first design of general-purpose computer.
Pascal's Adding machine was the first calculator or adding machine to be produced and actually used.

24. (b) The first graphical computer game was known as Baby. Pascal's calculator was an automatic mechanical device.
IBM 650 was the first mass produced computer. Cray-1 was developed by Los Alamos National Lab.

25. (b) Transistors were used in first generation where magnetic drum was used for storage and instructions were in machine language. Vacuum tubes were used in second generation where magnetic tape was used for storage and high level PC like FORTRAN was the language used.

26. (b) In third generation, ICs were used. The memory used in these computers was the large magnetic core, magnetic disk or tape.

CHAPTER 3

1. (a)	**2.** (b)	**3.** (b)	**4.** (a)	**5.** (b)
6. (c)	**7.** (c)	**8.** (d)	**9.** (b)	**10.** (c)
11. (b)	**12.** (a)	**13.** (d)	**14.** (d)	**15.** (c)
16. (c)	**17.** (b)	**18.** (a)	**19.** (b)	**20.** (c)
21. (d)	**22.** (d)	**23.** (d)	**24.** (d)	**25.** (a)
26. (b)	**27.** (b)	**28.** (b)	**29.** (a)	**30.** (b)
31. (b)	**32.** (a)	**33.** (b)	**34.** (b)	**35.** (d)
36. (b)	**37.** (c)			

38. (d) Hardware interacts with OS and can be touched and felt. User is the one who interacts with the software and is unaware of the background working.
39. (a) Sequential Access Memory (SAM) stores data in a sequence. Non-Sequential Memory has data in random order.
40. (d) None of these

    Memory is what your computer uses to store data temporarily, while storage is where you save files permanently.

    Memory allows processor to access data to run various applications and switch b/w them while storage allows storing and accessing files and applications.

    Memory is volatile but fast while storage is non-volatile but slow.
41. (d) Function keys cause an operating system command interpreter or application program to perform specific task.

    e.g. F1 key is often used as the default 'Help key' in many program.

    F5 key is used in an Internet Browser to refresh or reload a web page.

    The function of these keys can differ with each OS and s/w program.
42. (d) Storage is a mechanism that enables a computer to retain data, either temporarily or permanently. And speaker is a output device.
43. (b)
    (A) RAM is type of volatile memory.
    (B) Motherboard contains major components of a computer.
    (C) Scanner is input device whereas projector is output device.
    (D) MS Word is an application software that allows us to design, edit and work upon a text file.

CHAPTER 4

1. (b)	**2.** (d)	**3.** (c)	**4.** (a)	**5.** (b)
6. (b)	**7.** (b)	**8.** (b)	**9.** (c)	**10.** (a)
11. (b)	**12.** (c)	**13.** (b)	**14.** (b)	**15.** (b)
16. (c)	**17.** (d)	**18.** (d)	**19.** (d)	**20.** (a)
21. (b)	**22.** (a)	**23.** (a)	**24.** (b)	**25.** (a)
26. (c)	**27.** (d)	**28.** (b)		

29. (b) Aero shake allows users to minimise unwanted open windows. It works by shaping it bi-directionally.
30. (c) My Lockbox provides an option to lock files and apps. It also has exceptional rules to execute certain files and programs.
31. (b) Safe mode starts windows with a limited set of drivers and files.
32. (c) Cortana can be opened by right click on the taskbar button and click on show cortana.

CHAPTER 5

1. (c)	**2.** (a)	**3.** (a)	**4.** (c)	**5.** (b)
6. (d)	**7.** (a)	**8.** (b)	**9.** (d)	**10.** (c)
11. (b)	**12.** (c)	**13.** (a)	**14.** (a)	**15.** (c)
16. (a)	**17.** (a)	**18.** (c)	**19.** (b)	**20.** (b)
21. (b)				

22. (b) The given pictures represent envelope, labels and mail merge.
23. (d) When we click on the select recipients in mail merge, then we get the drop-down list.
24. (c) A Gutter Margin adds extra space to the side margin, top margin, or inside margins of a document that you plan to bind. It helps ensure that text isn't obscured by the binding.
25. (c) Drop cap is a large capital letter. To insert it, we can select a particular paragraph. Then click on insert, then go to text section and click on the drop cap option and select desired option in list.
26. (b) To add line number, click on the Page Layout tab. Then, click on line numbers button in page set up option. A drop-down menu appears. Select the required option.
27. (a) The chart type can be changed by using Design tab from Chart tools.
28. (d) The description of chart on any side is known as legends.
29. (c) Mailings tab has all the options that are required by an E-mail.
30. (c) Ctrl+N is used to create shortcut for a new document.

    Pressing F8 3 times selects a sentence

    Alt + F + A is used to open dialog box

    The Tab key moves to the next cell in MS Word.
31. (d) Start mode is used to insert a page break.

CHAPTER 6

1. (a) **2.** (d) **3.** (b) **4.** (c) **5.** (d)
6. (c) **7.** (b) **8.** (c) **9.** (a) **10.** (d)
11. (b) **12.** (c) **13.** (b) **14.** (c) **15.** (d)
16. (d) **17.** (b) **18.** (d) **19.** (b)

20. (a) To add a name to our worksheet, we need to go to formulas option then, go to defined names tab and there we can define a name.

21. (a) **22.** (b)

23. (c) If we double click a cell, we can insert or delete its data.

24. (c) Σ is used for autosum function. It can also calculate the average, minimum and maximum values.

25. (a) To quickly access details of a name, we can type the name in the name box. Font box is used to change the font.

26. (a) To change the background of an excel sheet, we should first select the current sheet then, choose page layout then, page set up and then, background to add a image to background of worksheet.

27. (d) We can protect a worksheet as well as a workbook.

28. (d) Selection Pane in Excel is used to arrange the objects on a worksheet.

29. (a) Ctrl+C copies the data and Ctrl+V is used to paste it.
Ctrl+9 hides a selected row.
Ctrl+shift+9 to unhide any hidden rows.
Alt+A is used to open the data tab.

30. (c)
(A) Ω is used to insert symbols.
(B) *fx* is used to insert any functions.
(C) Represents all the views of a workbook in Excel.
(D) There are different types of charts that can be inserted in a worksheet.

CHAPTER 7

1. (c) **2.** (b) **3.** (a) **4.** (d) **5.** (a)
6. (c) **7.** (a) **8.** (c) **9.** (a) **10.** (b)
11. (c) **12.** (b) **13.** (b) **14.** (a) **15.** (b)
16. (c) **17.** (b) **18.** (a) **19.** (c) **20.** (b)
21. (b) **22.** (c) **23.** (a) **24.** (b) **25.** (b)
26. (a) **27.** (c) **28.** (c) **29.** (a)

30. (a) Notes page allows us to view the Notes written at the bottom of each slide. We can also print the Notes to later use them as reference.

31. (a) Handouts are a summary of the presentation. It has all the slides and a brief description of them.

32. (b) The narration of a slide can be recorded and we can also rehearse our presentation to get an idea of the time taken to deliver the presentation using these features.

33. (a) Alt+N takes the cursor to Insert tab.
Alt+H changes the layout of the slides. We can go to the next slide using Page Down key. To cut an object, slide etc; we use Ctrl+X.

34. (d) Fourth icon represents animations that can be worked with in PowerPoint.

CHAPTER 8

1. (b) **2.** (d) **3.** (a) **4.** (c) **5.** (d)
6. (c) **7.** (a) **8.** (d) **9.** (b) **10.** (c)
11. (d) **12.** (d) **13.** (b) **14.** (d) **15.** (c)
16. (d) **17.** (a) **18.** (d) **19.** (d) **20.** (d)
21. (b) **22.** (c) **23.** (c) **24.** (c)

25. (d) "?" will give the combined output of Seema Deepak 1222.

26. (b) It is necessary to begin each program with SET command and TERMINATE it. "?" is used in QBASIC to print the output.

27. (c) QBASIC has less storage and number of functions.
QBASIC has limited storage and number of functions.

28. (d) Since, we have given print commands for A$, D$ and F$, therefore, only 'HELLO ARE YOU' will be printed.

CHAPTER 9

1. (c) **2.** (b) **3.** (c) **4.** (a) **5.** (b)
6. (a) **7.** (b) **8.** (a) **9.** (d) **10.** (b)
11. (c) **12.** (d) **13.** (b) **14.** (c) **15.** (b)
16. (d) **17.** (a) **18.** (c) **19.** (d) **20.** (d)
21. (a) **22.** (c) **23.** (d) **24.** (b) **25.** (a)

26. (d) **27.** (b) **28.** (b) **29.** (c) **30.** (a)

31. (c) Blind Carbon Copy (BCC) hides a certain recipient name.

32. (b) Modem generally uses a telephone line and provides modulation and demodulation.

33. (a) Gmail is main service provided by Google. It is not an E-commerce website.

34. (c) An organisation has internal network known as Intranet. ARPANET was also an Intranet.

35. (c) WWW (World Wide Web) was developed by Tim Berners Lee.

Wireless PAN is personal network that allows bluetooth connections.

BSNL is Bharat Sanchar Nigam Limited. It is an Indian Service Provider.

Facebook is a social networking site.

CHAPTER 10

1. (c) **2.** (a) **3.** (d) **4.** (c) **5.** (b)
6. (d) **7.** (c) **8.** (b) **9.** (d) **10.** (c)
11. (d) **12.** (c) **13.** (c) **14.** (b) **15.** (d)
16. (c) **17.** (b) **18.** (b) **19.** (a)

20. (c) Kiosk is a small, free standing structure which can be digital or non-digital. It can be found at different places.

21. (c) Iris recognition system is one of the recent and most secure authentication service. It scans the retina and matches it with the database.

22. (b) Xbox is very popular home video game console developed by Microsoft.

23. (b) The given icon is of MS Office365 Suite which provides all MS Office applications.

24. (a) **25.** (c)

Practice Set 1

1.	(b)	**2.**	(c)	**3.**	(c)	**4.**	(b)	**5.**	(a)	**6.**	(c)	**7.**	(b)	**8.**	(c)	**9.**	(b)	**10.**	(b)
11.	(d)	**12.**	(c)	**13.**	(d)	**14.**	(b)	**15.**	(c)	**16.**	(d)	**17.**	(d)	**18.**	(c)	**19.**	(b)	**20.**	(d)
21.	(a)	**22.**	(b)	**23.**	(c)	**24.**	(b)	**25.**	(a)	**26.**	(d)	**27.**	(a)	**28.**	(d)	**29.**	(b)	**30.**	(b)
31.	(d)	**32.**	(d)	**33.**	(b)	**34.**	(d)	**35.**	(c)	**36.**	(d)	**37.**	(b)	**38.**	(d)	**39.**	(a)	**40.**	(b)
41.	(d)	**42.**	(d)	**43.**	(a)	**44.**	(b)	**45.**	(b)	**46.**	(b)	**47.**	(b)	**48.**	(a)	**49.**	(c)	**50.**	(b)

Practice Set 2

1.	(a)	**2.**	(d)	**3.**	(d)	**4.**	(c)	**5.**	(a)	**6.**	(b)	**7.**	(d)	**8.**	(b)	**9.**	(d)	**10.**	(b)
11.	(c)	**12.**	(a)	**13.**	(b)	**14.**	(a)	**15.**	(b)	**16.**	(b)	**17.**	(a)	**18.**	(c)	**19.**	(c)	**20.**	(c)
21.	(b)	**22.**	(d)	**23.**	(d)	**24.**	(a)	**25.**	(c)	**26.**	(b)	**27.**	(d)	**28.**	(d)	**29.**	(a)	**30.**	(b)
31.	(b)	**32.**	(c)	**33.**	(a)	**34.**	(b)	**35.**	(a)	**36.**	(d)	**37.**	(c)	**38.**	(d)	**39.**	(b)	**40.**	(b)
41.	(b)	**42.**	(c)	**43.**	(c)	**44.**	(d)	**45.**	(c)	**46.**	(a)	**47.**	(b)	**48.**	(a)	**49.**	(d)	**50.**	(a)

Practice Set 3

1.	(b)	**2.**	(b)	**3.**	(d)	**4.**	(b)	**5.**	(a)	**6.**	(b)	**7.**	(b)	**8.**	(d)	**9.**	(b)	**10.**	(c)
11.	(d)	**12.**	(c)	**13.**	(c)	**14.**	(a)	**15.**	(b)	**16.**	(c)	**17.**	(b)	**18.**	(d)	**19.**	(a)	**20.**	(c)
21.	(a)	**22.**	(a)	**23.**	(d)	**24.**	(d)	**25.**	(b)	**26.**	(d)	**27.**	(c)	**28.**	(c)	**29.**	(b)	**30.**	(d)
31.	(d)	**32.**	(d)	**33.**	(c)	**34.**	(c)	**35.**	(b)	**36.**	(c)	**37.**	(d)	**38.**	(b)	**39.**	(d)	**40.**	(b)
41.	(d)	**42.**	(c)	**43.**	(c)	**44.**	(d)	**45.**	(b)	**46.**	(c)	**47.**	(d)	**48.**	(c)	**49.**	(a)	**50.**	(d)

www.ingramcontent.com/pod-product-compliance
Ingram Content Group UK Ltd.
Pitfield, Milton Keynes, MK11 3LW, UK
UKHW050137280726
14058UKWH00006B/696